Banking on the Biosphere?

Banking on the Biosphere?

Environmental Procedures and Practices of Nine Multilateral Development Agencies

Robert E. Stein

Brian Johnson
The International Institute for
Environment and Development

Lexington Books
D. C. Heath and Company
Lexington, Massachusetts
Toronto

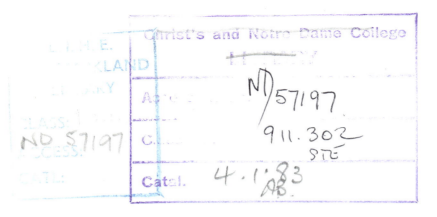

Library of Congress Cataloging in Publication Data

Main entry under title:

Banking on the biosphere?

   Report of a study conducted by the International Institute for
Environment and Development.
   Bibliography: p.
   Includes index.
   1. Economics assistance—Environmental aspects. 2. Technical assis-
tance—Environmental aspects. 3. Development banks—Environmental as-
pects. I. Stein, Robert E. II. Johnson, Brian D.G. III. International Insti-
tute for Environment and Development.
HC60.B2697   301.31   78-24123
ISBN 0-669-02734-0

Contents

List of Tables

Foreword

We have been impressed by abundant evidence that this survey of the relationship between nine international development financing institutions and the human and natural environment which are affected by their projects is timely. This has been made clear by the interest and enthusiasm that has been encountered in the course of this research. Indeed we are confident that our undertaking of this study has affected all the agencies studied in a generally positive way, raising the consciousness of officials and helping them to reexamine many conventional ideas and assumptions about development.

We have, not surprisingly, uncovered many voids in perception about environmental impacts and a general absence (with the partial exception of the World Bank) of systematic attention to environmental impacts of all stages of project conception, design, and execution.

One important caveat, though, should be made at the outset. The findings of this survey are based not upon field research but upon detailed discussions with agency officials and on access to a limited range of documents. We are convinced, however, that this basis has provided us with an adequate picture to show the lines of urgently needed change. The fact that the finger of accusation is not here pointed sharply at particular institutions or projects, but the positive approach taken of affirming the better examples of practice, does not mean that we fail to recognize environmental catastrophes associated with development projects and many lesser past and current mistakes and misdirections. It is rather that we believe that the problems tend to speak for themselves. What has been too little considered and spoken about are viable solutions and necessary changes of tactics. We are convinced that this approach is what gives our report its special timeliness and relevance to policy makers.

Barbara Ward
(Baroness Jackson of Lodsworth)
Sussex, England

Preface

This study of attitudes and approaches to the environment among a group of international development financing institutions was conducted in the course of 1977.[a] Readers wishing to examine the precise terms of reference of the study and the methodology employed, and readers less familiar with the structure and membership of the institutions concerned should turn to appendixes A to J.

The modesty of this study's range and depth should be stressed at the outset. Neither resources nor time permitted field trips to look at projects or to conduct in-depth case studies. Moreover, the projects that were examined in some depth (through documentary review and interviews) could not be discussed here at any length without either disturbing the balance of a comparative study of nine institutions, or rendering this report too long and diffuse to be useful to busy people. This study, then, is more in the nature of a survey. But it is hoped that sufficient analysis was possible to offer some valid conclusions. These, necessarily tentative as the area of activity covered here is vast, are drawn together in chapter 10.

Throughout the study the delicacy of the relationship between a development assistance agency and a sovereign government to which it lends or makes grants was kept in mind. The authors were repeatedly reminded that such development agencies are neither willing nor able to impose specific environmental requirements upon a government if that government is unpersuaded of the wisdom or appropriateness of the requirement. Indeed, several cases were encountered where loan requests were withdrawn because of what a government regarded as excessive insistence by an agency on a particular approach to a problem.

The constraints on insistence are very real. At the same time instances were observed to occur where development banks hesitate to commit funds because they are concerned about the environmental soundness of a particular national request. On the basis of the projects examined and the personnel interviewed, it seems clear that there is a great deal that can be done in modification and redirection of a grant or loan project if the lending institution offers appropriate technical advice at the right moment, and if the process of negotiation is kept positive. As this report reveals, experience certainly shows that offers of help by aid agencies to ensure environmental soundness in projects are generally welcomed by recipient governments, if they avoid excessive interference with governments' development priorities and do not threaten to slow down their development process.

---

[a]The institutions were: African Development Bank (ADB); Arab Bank for Economic Development of Africa (BADEA); Asian Development Bank (AsDB); Caribbean Development Bank (CDB); European Development Bank (EDF); Inter-American Development Bank (IDB); International Bank for Reconstruction and Development (IBRD or World Bank); Organization of American States (OAS); and United Nations Development Programme (UNDP).

Throughout this survey the authors were also kept aware that the environmental impact which multilateral development agencies can have on national development is generally modest when compared to the scale of the national development effort, and indeed the scale of other external investment, official and private, which helps to shape the development priorities of a country. Nevertheless, a number of instances were encountered in which the policies and practices of these development institutions have had a catalytic effect on the formulation of national developmental activities. The extent to which these international institutions may exert a positive environmental influence depends very much, of course, on the level of environmental consciousness in these agencies, the degree of precision with which they have formulated their environmental concern, the extent to which they have translated general environmental perceptions into sectoral policies, and how far they have gone in training personnel in this dimension of development thinking.

Naturally wide variations were found among the institutions surveyed in all these matters. This report devotes a great deal more space to the International Bank for Reconstruction and Development (the World Bank) than to any of the other institutions surveyed. This is not simply because of the Bank's preeminence as a lender, disbursing as it does in a year considerably more than all of the other institutions examined put together. More important is the fact that the World Bank has shown, since the early 1970s, a unique practical concern over the environmental impact of its lending. This record is examined critically. The authors also have looked for ways in which other multilateral development financing institutions may learn from World Bank experience, both positive and negative. Indeed, the authors also hope that one of the major uses to which this survey may be put is to help these institutions to achieve greater interaction on environmental policy and practice among each other.

It is also hoped that the tentative conclusions arrived at in the International Institute for Environment and Development's Interim Report on Work in Progress (September 1977) are sufficiently supported and modified by findings here in four substantive fields of activity for them to form the basis of a dialogue on the subject of environmental impact within the development community: one which will involve not only the institutions surveyed in the following pages, but other multilateral and bilateral agencies both public and private.[b]

It seems that conceptual work on the relationship of environment and development has now been carried forward far enough to form the basis for such a dialogue. What is needed now is to get the concepts discussed among economists, engineers, planners, and loan officers of development banks both national and international. Only then will sound environmental practice be introduced on a scale and at a pace commensurate with the need for action.

---

[b]Such a dialogue seems to have been initiated at the Inter-American Development Bank, when the IDB invited representatives of the World Bank, the OAS, the UN Environment Programme, US Agency for International Development, and other public and private groups to participate in an open discussion with its staff and directors on environmental policies for the Bank to consider.

Acknowledgments

Carrying out a project such as this requires the support of a large number of people and institutions. We have received help from a variety of sources. The United Nations Environment Programme (UNEP) and the Canadian International Development Agency (CIDA) funded the project, and their resources made it possible to make at least one visit to each of the institutions under study. Because of limited time and resources we were unable to spend extended periods at the agencies, to visit projects in the field, or in some instances to revisit agency headquarters.

Of all those whose assistance made this project possible, we would particularly like to thank the many officials and members of the staffs of various development institutions who spent so much of their valuable time in discussions with us, and for their detailed comments on drafts of the study.

We appreciate the generous support given by the Human Settlements Project of the International Institute for Environment and Development (IIED), funded by the Ministry of Housing and Urban Affairs of Canada, which enabled us to expand our researches into human settlements projects further than would otherwise have been possible.

We would also like to thank the IIED Project Advisory Group (see appendix H), members of which were most helpful with suggestions and comments.

It remains to express our gratitude to Mae Dell Dulaney for her long hours and cheerful disposition in preparation of the manuscript, and to add that while we have been greatly assisted by those who helped us, the final responsibility for the study resides with the IEED Assessment Project Team.

Part I
Nine Multilateral Aid
Agencies

1 International Aid Agencies, Development, and the Environment: The Practical Impact of Some Unresolved Debates

The effect of international development aid programs on the environment is a subject of increasing interest and debate within and outside development agencies. The debate is of more than purely intellectual interest. It is having a practical impact on the policies and programs of these institutions, and on public attitudes towards their work.

An obvious first reason for this interest and the intensity of the current debate, is the scale of the spending involved. Over $27 billion was committed in 1976 as aid from governmental, intergovernmental, or international aid programs.[1] The environmental impact of this $27 billion is indeed much larger than the sum implies. It is larger because the bulk of these funds are matched by counterpart financing by the recipient country. It is larger still because a considerable slice of this money is spent on technical assistance, on planning, on training, and on research. So the multiplier is not only quantitative but qualitative: the programs financed by development aid agencies will influence the thinking and shape the skills and capacities of people whose decisions will be affecting the environment decades from now.

The Development Debate: The Choice of Development Pattern

This brief discussion of the environment-development relationship must begin with a summary of the current debate over development priorities, because the nature of environmental concern varies with the position adopted over these priorities.

It seems safe to say that until the early part of the present decade, few development authorities seriously questioned the proposition that Third World development should embrace the most rapid possible replication or reproduction of the industrial development of the advanced Northern economies. Within this paradigm arguments centered on priorities among sectors, but the general objective was clear.

It is clear no longer. It is not that industrialization itself has been questioned as a target (it certainly has not been in any government or intergovernmental development agency) but the pattern of industrialism by present strategies and

3

the nature of the technologies that it employs is widely under critical examination. The notion that presently poor countries must follow rich societies up the familiar industrial ladder is increasingly challenged. High and wasteful resource consumption, heavy dependence on dwindling nonrenewable resources (especially oil), massive migration into huge conurbations, the constant replacement by capital of a labor force which must seek opportunities in the new areas of dynamic industrial or postindustrial growth—this development pattern is now increasingly seen as unsustainable in rich and poor countries alike. This general concern and questioning is to be found in multilateral development assistance agencies, as elsewhere.

In the institutions surveyed, an increasing number of officials, especially younger ones, recognize that development of the kind actively promoted by their organizations has benefited relatively few people. They also tend to accept that this pattern is not sustainable in the future, particularly for developing countries, based as it is on extensive use of dwindling resources, preeminently oil.

These criticisms of the industrial ladder of development have the curious quality of being radical and at the same time commonplace within the institutions visited. This, in itself, indicates the confusion and turmoil that exist among practitioners of development: engineers, economists, scientists, and above all politicians and planners. The present state of uncertainty, felt almost tangibly in the offices visited, is not only a welcome sign of potential flexibility. It may, like the churning of long-compacted soil, offer fertile opportunities for the seeds of new ideas.

Yet development financing institutions tend to be conservative bodies, often slow to respond to changing circumstances and new ideas. Their commitment to finance the traditional pattern of projects has by no means been abandoned. Indeed it is kept forcefully in being by the legitimate desire of most, if not all, developing nations to enter the modern global economy as effectively and quickly as possible. This commitment continues to cause the bulk of multilateral aid funds to be channeled to investments in "modernization" and infrastructure, particularly to electrical power generation and distribution and to modern transportation systems.

The Environmental Dimension of Traditional
Development Patterns

It is encouraging to note that nearly all of the multilateral aid institutions have by now recognized, at least in theory, the need for environmental protection measures to be applied to their modern-sector activities. This is particularly true of measures to protect against pollution and health hazards in crowded areas, even though established policies and procedures to ensure such protection are still generally lacking. Indeed, the need for environmental protection is no longer subject to widespread debate, though there is still a good deal of practical resistance. Opposition to these measures (sporadic and uneven in quality though they still are) has to be overcome both within the institutions themselves, and, more importantly, within some developing countries where these controls are often interpreted as unnecessary restrictions on their industrial growth. More recently, a growing recognition in the developing countries themselves of the value of pollution control and environmental health protection has begun to counter much of the criticism.

However, for many people interviewed in the institutions visited, their concept of environmental protection still involves either an elitist commitment to conservation, or relatively simple matters of industrial pollution controls. Any quest for broader environmental awareness to take account of resource and environmental management appears to be either unrealistic utopianism or an undesirable and unnecessary addition to their already heavy workloads. For these people, especially the older staff, set in established habits of project formulation, reference to the environment establishes the presumption of a narrowly bounded discussion. Many who do accept the importance of environmental protection nevertheless hesitate to assign it sufficient priority to have a practical impact on their work.

Since the 1972 Stockholm Conference on the Human Environment, this debate over the priority to be given to environmental protection in developing countries has taken place in the shadow of an animated discussion in which many have actually equated poverty with pollution. This debate has been continuing in the development community at large and in United Nations fora. According to those who link environmental concern closely with poverty, poor people, especially those belonging to rapidly expanding communities, inevitably overtax the sustaining power of their already impoverished environments. Poverty thus inevitably breeds pollution and proliferates environmental destruction. Environmentally sound development is seen by this side in the debate as resource development for human purposes which does not irreversibly undermine or destroy any resource base on which man's life and well-being depends, and which benefits all people and is sustainable in the long run. The opposing view is that to equate pollution with poverty is either merely to introduce definitional confusion at an almost theological level of abstraction, or a rather unsubtle attempt to divert resources from one area of priority concern to another.

There is no need here to attempt to resolve the question of whether poverty may be equated with pollution. The value of the debate, however, is that it maintains the focus of argument on the issue of poverty while directing discussion to the fact that sound development is totally dependent on a sustaining environment. This debate is also closely related to, indeed is a part of, the more substantive debate over the priority to be given to basic needs.

The Basic Needs Debate

Since the early 1970s (partly, but not predominantly, because of environmental considerations) a new priority of development thinking has emerged, to some extent in all these institutions, but particularly in the World Bank. In response to public criticism that development aid was only benefiting a fortunate (and generally urban) elite, a new strategy of development aimed at the world's poorest people has gradually evolved. Though it remains vague and uncodified, this new strategy puts emphasis on finding ways to meet acute human needs. Instead of waiting for the benefits of modern sector growth to reach the very poor (which they have shown little, if any sign of doing), some development banks and aid agencies have accepted the challenge—at least as official policy—of directing development aid resources and services directly to the most urgent needs of the indigent in both rural and urban areas. Under this strategy, agricultural development (other than irrigation), education and health facilities for the poorest sectors of society, agricultural feeder roads, and, more recently, broadly conceived integrated rural development projects are given much higher priority. However, precept has far outpaced practice, and remarkably few of these projects, outside of the World Bank, have so far left the drawing board.

It is clear that the institutions studied, whatever their official policy positions, are not ready yet to give high priority to programs designed to provide assistance to the poorest sectors of developing societies. A trend in that direction, although gaining force in some sectors, is impeded by the great technical, institutional, and human difficulties involved in implementing such projects: by their low rate of return and by increasingly vocal resistance from developing country governments. This last factor is emerging with increasing strength.

Third World governments often resent basic needs priorities as one more example of imperial tutelage, while seeing them as diverting both scarce foreign currency aid and national counterpart resources away from projects which may accumulate savings faster, and hence prepare a springboard for later rapid growth. They argue that traditional development projects could benefit the whole population and may also prove a more rapid route to national independence and to increasing the country's status and power.

The Environment and Basic Needs Strategies

Only in the World Bank, and to some extent in the U.N. Development Programme, has strong conceptual and practical support for a "basic needs" strategy appeared at the highest policy levels. Even there it is not always endorsed or followed through in redirected patterns of lending. It is thus probably no coincidence that only in the World Bank can an observer identify serious support for the concept that there is a close, mutually supporting relationship between environmental concern and development priorities. Indeed, the Bank's official definition of environment takes account of the broad view of "environment" which has been articulated by many politicians and sociologists from developing countries. The World Bank identifies two different kinds of environmental problems: the effects of poverty and the effects of economic development. As Dr. James Lee, Director of the Bank's Office of Environmental and Health Affairs (OEHA), has put it:

> Under conditions of poverty, the biophysical environment often exhibits the ravages of long years of mismanagement (over-grazing, erosion, denuded forests, surface water pollution, etc.). Not merely the "quality" of life but life itself is endangered for it is often very difficult and sometimes impossible for the environment to renew its life supporting capabilities. Developing countries assign the highest priority to finding solutions to problems of this nature. Here the principal concern is to rehabilitate the environment that has gone through a long period of deterioration.

> The other set of problems accompanies the process of development itself. Agricultural growth, for example, calls for construction of irrigation and drainage systems, clearing of forests, use of fertilisers and pesticides—all of which have environmental and health implications. Similarly, the process of industrialisation could well result in the release of pollutants and in other environmental problems related to the extraction and processing of raw materials.[2]

At the World Bank, and also in some national aid programs, there is an increasingly clear understanding that development institutions must concentrate on development strategies (particularly in the case of projects intended to serve the poor directly) that are sustainable over more than the short run. To be sustainable, under this policy, development must be environmentally sound in the broadest sense.

"Sustainable development" is not often publicly articulated as an objective, probably because a development project's sustainability is too often—wrongly—assumed. Certainly the concept is not much explored in development literature. It hinges on the belief (or calculation) that environmentally unsound projects—projects that fail to account for their environmental side-effects (like lake siltation, soil salination, and the spread of water-borne diseases) or that overtax or pollute a resource base (like ill-sited or ill-equipped industrial projects), or that fail to protect the health of workers—will not prove economically, let alone socially, acceptable in anything but the shortest run.

If sustainability as a criterion for sound development is given only token acceptance, even by many World Bank officials and staff, it has received much less attention in the other multilateral aid institutions studied. The regional banks have officially said very little about the relationship between poverty, development, and environmental degradation. This may indicate a lack of perception of, or concern with, the long-term future more often than outright opposition. But outright opposition exists, too, among those who argue that modernization can continue to rely on the latest technological innovation to outstrip resource depletion and to abate pollution. Such views face, however, an unresolved dilemma between ever greater dependence on more sophisticated technologies and the external dependence which such reliance may perpetuate.

The Debate on Alternative Technology

Argument over the priority to be given to appropriate technologies is clearly inseparable from both the "basic needs" and "poverty is pollution" debates. Obviously the concept of appropriate technology can embrace a wide variety of development values and strategies. Almost everyone recognizes the utility of transfers of some advanced technologies from the industrial world. But increasingly the use of simpler tools and solutions, renewable energy resources, labor rather than capital intensive projects, and resource-conserving devices is advocated. Many of the banks surveyed here have begun to favor appropriate technology methods and solutions in ongoing projects. This trend seems generally to be beneficent from an environmental point of view. The inherent environmental beneficence of simpler or more labor intensive technology should not, however, be assumed prima facie as too often is the case. Yet even within the international development banks, and particularly in some developing countries, the concept of appropriate technology is still often bracketed with basic needs strategies and suspected as a ploy of the industrialized countries to block one of the aims of the new international economic order—the transfer of modern technology on concessional terms to the developing world. In practical terms it is questionable whether these disagreements either delay or hasten the painfully slow pace of the search for technologies appropriate to specific development strategies. Certainly the role of the nine multilateral aid institutions in promoting appropriate technologies has so far been limited and unfocused.

The Role of Multilateral Development
Financing Institutions

Naturally these debates on concepts of development and the relationship of development to environment involve major differences over the social, economic, and political objectives of development. And these debates are further reflected in disagreements over the nature of the multilateral aid organizations themselves: should they be primarily financial institutions or primarily development agencies? To what extent should they seek to be, or allow themselves to become, agents of social and political change in the developing world? To the extent that a multilateral aid organization is a predominantly financial institution, how much should it concern itself with environmental questions rather than leaving these to the developing country? Again, these large questions cannot be resolved in a study such as this. But again, too, judgment on attitudes and approaches in these agencies (which are inevitable and occur implicitly and explicitly throughout this report) *must* be made if analysis is to be followed by any recommendations for positive action.

A Framework for Examination of the Banks' Environmental Practices

What importance do the considerations discussed in this chapter have as a framework for examining the environmental policies and practices of the multilateral development financing institutions? Is it necessary to define environment or environmental protection, or to redefine development to assess the work of the banks? Although it is useful, and even important, to consider all aspects of the continuing debate, clear conclusions on these issues, or lasting all-purpose definitions of such broad terms, must remain elusive. Nor are they essential to the aims of this report. Both sides of the opposed arguments must always be borne in mind. They will continually influence the allocation of resources and the pattern of both development and environmental protection both for governments and international funding agencies.

For the purposes of this study one point is clear: the value of examining the banks' environmental policies and practices does not depend on resolving, even temporarily, the continuing debate, nor any of its parts. Nor does it necessarily depend on accepting the absolute priority of any of the principles so warmly debated, even though recognition of their importance is valuable in clarifying what is happening and what ought to happen in these institutions.

It seems enough at this stage to put forward four relatively simple and broadly accepted criteria regarding development and environment as guideposts for this study. First, one objective at least of development must be the meeting of critical human needs. Secondly, the needs of future generations must be protected. Thirdly, international developmental institutions, more specifically the development banks studied here, have a responsibility to propose and encourage the modification of projects that would otherwise harm the health or quality of life of affected peoples, or would unacceptably deplete (admittedly often a subjective question) resources, or harm physical systems on which man's welfare—in the longer run even his fate—depends. Finally, these institutions should consider reorienting their programs, and consequently their projects, to reflect a more conserving use of resources and a more sustainable form of development.

Notes

1. About one third of this round total was committed by the nine institutions reviewed in this report.

2. Dr. James A. Lee, "Environment and Development: The World Bank Experience" (Paper presented at an international briefing sponsored by the Centre for International Environmental Information, New York, October 14, 1976) pp. 6-7. Reprinted with permission.

2 The World Bank

The sheer scale of the World Bank's operations sets it qualitatively as well as quantitatively apart from the other aid agencies covered by this study.[1] In fiscal year 1977, new financial commitments of the World Bank (IBRD and IDA) exceeded $7 billion U.S. dollars.[2] Adding the commitments of the International Finance Corporation, the total approaches $7.3 billion—well over a quarter of the aid committed from all official sources. By the end of fiscal year 1977, accumulated World Bank operations involved over 2,100 projects in 116 developing countries, representing a total Bank investment of $50 billion. Of this, $24.1 billion has been authorized since 1974, funding a total of 806 projects. Apart from the unmatched size of its lending program, the World Bank is unique in the global reach of its operations. No regional development bank, and few if any national aid organizations have had to address as broad a range of problems as the World Bank has been forced to consider by virtue of its worldwide activities.

The World Bank has the most advanced environmental policy and practices of any aid organization included in this study and undoubtedly exerts intellectual leadership on environmental matters in the entire international development community. The Bank's annual report for 1977 claims that "Every project is now routinely examined for its environmental implications (including health), and any protective measures, identified as necessary, are incorporated into its design and execution."[3] This commitment to environmental soundness in development has not always been so thorough, but has received continuing attention over the past eight years, and shows every sign of being an increasingly important aspect of the Bank's work.

Nature and Sources of the Bank's Environmental Commitment

The first formal commitment to environmental soundness in development came when the World Bank set up the Office of Environmental Adviser in 1970,[4] although there was no high-level policy statement on the subject until President Robert S. McNamara addressed the Stockholm Conference on the Human Environment in 1972. By that date, the post of environmental adviser had been in existence about eighteen months. McNamara described the dilemma which led to the creation of the new post:

11

> The question is not whether there should be continued economic growth. There must be. Nor is the question whether the impact on the environment must be respected. It has to be. Nor—least of all—is it a question of whether these two considerations are interlocked. They are.
>
> The solution of the dilemma revolves clearly not about whether, but about how.[5]

The World Bank overcame considerable initial resistance to its environmental concern among developing countries, principally by acceding to the concept of additionality, which required that the Bank provide funds to cover any additional costs directly attributable to its environmental standards. There has never been a protest lodged formally because of the imposition of environmentally motivated modifications, although in negotiations the issues can become quite complicated.[6] The Bank has actually balked on occasion at funding environmental safeguards that it deems unnecessary or overly sophisticated.

As noted in the preceding chapter, the World Bank decided to adopt a very broad definition of environment. But it should also be noted that the Bank's official concept of environmental problems does not yet include much discussion of the pattern of development, for example, decentralized agriculture and urban-centered industrial development. It is not that the World Bank is uninterested in these problems, but it tends to separate them from concepts of environmental impact.

The officially broad view of environment has not, however, prompted a correspondingly broad range of activities within the World Bank's Office of Environmental and Health Affairs (OEHA). Probably the decision taken in 1970, to focus first on the amelioration of adverse environmental effects of large-scale industrial projects, was pragmatically unavoidable. Useful results have certainly been achieved. For example, effluent emission criteria and occupational health and safety standards have been developed (though never codified and published) during the intervening years. However, the choice of emphasis has meant that OEHA has not been able to concentrate adequately on those environmental problems of degradation and poor resource management which developing countries have themselves identified as urgent.

Environmental Health and Human Ecologic Considerations in Economic Development Projects (1973) was the World Bank's first instructional document on environmental precaution,[7] which covered various environmentally sensitive areas of development. Some elements of environmentally sound practice (usually, however, not so identified) also began to be included in the Bank's sectoral papers. However, it was only in 1976 and 1977, with the preparation of the Rural Water Supply and Forestry Policy Papers by the Bank's project staff with major outside participation, that new policy directions built around sound environmental practice began to be incorporated into the Bank's basic policy documents, or that the process of formulating these policy documents became an important means of expanding the Bank's environmentally oriented programs and thinking. In time all of the Bank's influential sectoral policy papers need to be reviewed for the same purposes.

Functions of the Office of Environmental and Health Affairs

In principle, the OEHA is committed to a review, and where necessary the restructuring, of every project funded by the World Bank which has a significant environmental, health, or human ecological impact. The review function is entrusted principally to OEHA. In fact, although the small environmental group in OEHA only has time to screen closely a small part of the total flow of loan projects, it undoubtedly does succeed in isolating and, usually, in correcting offenders. The OEHA professional staff reviews project briefs and may select any given project for more careful scrutiny. The workload is awesome—one staff member said he had reviewed over one hundred projects in forty-five days and had made recommendations on sixty-five of them—and certain kinds of projects, especially industrial and water projects having notable health effects, tend to receive more of OEHA's attention than others. It appears that this heavy workload inevitably leads to occasional hurried and superficial judgments.

These OEHA review procedures inevitably rely heavily on the Bank staff's realization that a project must be able to pass environmental muster after appraisal ("appraisal" in the case of the World Bank marks the point at which a project's overall acceptability on most grounds is certified), because it is impossible for OEHA to become systematically involved in the earlier stages of project identification and preparation. Some efforts have been made to overcome this problem—for example, by occasionally sending out an "environmental reconnaissance" mission which occurs early enough to influence site selection and project design.

Indeed, the direct work of OEHA represents only one element of the Bank's environmental review. Project officers who have the primary responsibility for all aspects of a given project have the OEHA Environmental Handbook at their disposal. It first appeared in 1973, was revised and published in Spanish, French, and English in 1974, and is presently undergoing further revisions. Sectors covered include agriculture, industry, transportation, utilities, and public health. In the Bank's own words, the Handbook "has been designed to provide further guidance in the detection, identification and measurement of environmental and related human ecological effects."[8] The merits of this publication should not be underestimated; indeed, it has accurately been called "the first major effort of a lending institution to establish criteria for evaluating the environmental impact of its investment projects."[9] However, its importance may be in its innovative quality rather than in its overall effectiveness, particularly since it is necessarily written at a very general level and is not focused on the environmental circumstances and problems encountered in particular developing countries. In time it should be superseded, or at least supplemented, by more sophisticated documents dealing with various environmentally sensitive sectors which, unlike the guidelines, not only delineate the problems and how to avoid them, but also show how the environment may be improved or enhanced through appropriate choice of energy technology, forest management, soil conservation, better irrigation practice, and so forth.

The authors of this study concluded that one of OEHA's principal functions must be to prepare more sophisticated and specifically environmental handbooks, and to provoke and contribute to new environmentally sensitive sector papers. Not nearly enough of these have yet been done. Certainly new sector papers are needed in the areas of agricultural and rural development, fisheries, and pesticide uses, to mention obvious examples.

Another very important OEHA responsibility is the heightening of environmental consciousness and knowledge throughout the World Bank, particularly through training. Formally, this is done by occasional OEHA participation in Bank training activities. However, OEHA (and the Bank's top management) recognize that OEHA's staff is too small to undertake enough environmental training to meet the Bank's growing needs. The Bank badly needs to incorporate into the work of its Economic Development Institute (EDI) short courses specifically on environmental issues (particularly for new World Bank officers and for developers and planners from borrowing countries). In fact such an initiative appears to be imminent. Even more important is the production of well-conceived environmental content in all the courses and case studies used by the EDI.

Although many staff members of the World Bank in every department and office were interviewed during this study, it is still difficult to assess OEHA's success in performing this function. The work done by the Central Projects Staff (CPS), including the work of OEHA, is held in high regard by the staff of the regional offices. But when a staff member faces intense pressure to maintain a schedule for two or three large loans, "high regard" may be an insufficient inducement to take account of the proposals and requirements. One deputy director of a department pointed to a work table piled high with project documents for which he had direct responsibility, and asked how he could possibly be expected to stay abreast of advisory materials whose impact on projects might not be evident for years.

One problem arising from location of all environmental expertise in the Central Projects Staff is a degree of isolation whose ultimate impact is impossible to measure. For example, one major infrastructure project which had recently been appraised was reviewed. The particular plant to be built was to be located near one of the most badly polluted cities in the Third World, and would meet the government's existing pollution standards. The need for higher standards was a current political issue, and if these were imposed by the government, the borrower would incur substantial additional costs in order to qualify for a construction license. It was not contemplated that the Bank would cover these additional costs. The attitude of some members of the Bank's staff was that the borrower should not be burdened with unnecessarily sophisticated standards, particularly in an area that is already badly polluted. It did not seem to concern the Bank staff that a government which was considering grappling with a bad pollution problem would have to make a start somewhere, even if the initial effect of this effort would be minimal, or only marginally necessary in the case of this particular project.

This example serves to illustrate the difficulty of actually raising staff awareness. The staff members in question undoubtedly believed they were environmentally aware, which in their view meant that they had planned a project that met existing pollution standards. But advancing the larger purposes of the Bank's environmental policy apparently had not been uppermost in their minds in the course of the loan negotiation. A full OEHA review of all project documents would probably have revealed very little about the attitude with which Bank representatives approached the loan negotiations. Even if this project were approved as constituted at the time of this study, it would be grossly unfair to say that the OEHA had failed. The office simply has too few staff, too centrally located, to follow every aspect of the hundreds of projects under consideration at any one time.

Environmental Considerations and the Project Cycle

Environmental Procedures outside the OEHA

One of the principal environmental objectives of the World Bank is to ensure that sound environmental considerations are thoroughly incorporated into day-to-day thinking and practice. Each Bank official should automatically incorporate good environmental practice into his or her own work, which includes knowing when special environmental expertise should be summoned. This philosophy is highly commendable with one caution. As discussed below, project appraisal methodologies already treat the environment as an analytical component of the technical aspects of a project. The principle of "good environmental practice" becoming part of everyday Bank staff work is a potentially double-edged sword. That target should not be construed to mean that the environmental dimension of a project is not a subject worthy of separate, detailed consideration by experts.

Progress is already being made, due partly to the Bank's own efforts to heighten environmental consciousness, partly to increasing general professional understanding of environmental considerations, and partly to the arrival on the staff of younger officers who, because of their own education and experiences, have better background understanding of the environmental dimensions of development. All these conditions are still spread unevenly in various areas, but outright resistance to the idea that environmental concern (broadly defined to include the concept of sustainability) is crucial to sound development was rarely encountered.

The principal way in which environmental "good practice" is incorporated into the World Bank's work is, of course, through the planning and processing of loans. Some details as to just how environmental considerations are incorporated into the various stages of the Bank's project cycle are useful, precisely because this seems a good way to examine how environmental protection or enhancement is—or may best be—designed into every loan project. Technical details have been omitted here and the project cycle is discussed in general terms, principally to single out environmentally critical points in those considerations. In fact, what is said here also applies to the work of some of the other regional banks, who of necessity go through many of the same steps, and have in most cases taken World Bank procedures as their basic model. The project cycles of the World Bank and the Asian Development Bank (AsDB) are illustrated in appendix G).

Project Identification

The first step is to identify projects which could be financed by the World Bank. Theoretically this is the borrowing government's responsibility. But since many developing countries do not have the capability to carry it out themselves, the World Bank has become increasingly active in providing this service, particularly in connection with IDA loans. This is done routinely by sending missions to a country which will discuss that country's development objectives and its strategies for achieving them, and suggest areas where the Bank might help. Likewise, at times it looks at particular sectors of a country's—or several countries'—economy. An example is the recent West African forest sector survey which identified timber exploitation and forest management projects in a number of countries in West Africa. These country and sector missions are influential and frequently capable of pushing at least the externally financed part of a country's development plan in a certain direction.

Country Economic Missions (CEMs) are carried out annually or biannually to review borrower countries' overall economic condition and credit worthiness. Several years ago, senior bank staff debated, but rejected, the notion of expanding CEMs to be more general development planning missions, which would specifically have investigated environmental considerations. However, in the last several years, CEMs have been modified to reflect the "poorest of the poor" strategy, and their scope now includes topics such as rural and urban development, employment and income distribution, and population and human resources development.

Less well known outside the World Bank is the Country Program Paper (CPP), which is a brief strategy document prepared by the Bank to point out how it can assist a given country to achieve its development goals. The CPP may also discuss what the Bank should do to get a country to modify unrealistic, or poorly defined objectives. The few country economic papers and strategy papers reviewed for this report paid little or no attention to the resource and ecological problems and constraints which affect countries' developmental prospects. Either or both of these documents should include some assessment of a country's supply of critical resources needed to meet basic needs, and should encourage the evolution of strategies for land-use planning and the correction of critical cases of loss or degradation of resources. Finally, for purposes of environmental planning, the reports of country sector missions may be extremely significant, since these teams have ample opportunity to obtain detailed information, conduct discussions with government officials, and formulate policies geared specifically to local circumstances.

The OEHA has increasingly insisted on including in all of these missions Bank personnel and consultants knowledgeable about the environmental problems that a particular identification mission should single out. It is probably fair to say that, from an environmental viewpoint, the quality of the Bank personnel and consultants sent on these missions and the terms of reference under which they are dispatched is sporadic but improving. Largely because of the constraint of paying almost unique attention to financial and economic considerations, mission reports still rarely discuss environmental dimensions in enough detail. However, an increasing number of environmentally sensitive reports are now appearing, especially some of the recent reports on the Sahel and Nepal.

The inclusion of specific environmental sections in such reports is not advocated. Rather, short, intelligent discussions of the environmental limits within which a country must operate would be very useful, and the prospects for environmental development should be included and integrated into discussions of economic and social development objectives. If done sensitively, these papers could become powerful levers for lifting environmental awareness among both Bank personnel and borrowers. The latter, after all, must be one of the ultimate environmental missions of the World Bank.

Project Preparation

Once a project is identified as bankable and general agreement has been reached with the borrower that project design should go ahead, a short project brief is prepared to alert the appropriate Bank officials. This contains a short description of the project and sometimes outlines the problems which will be faced. The OEHA, which receives all project briefs, uses this document to alert itself to projects which are likely to pose environmental problems. Those among the project staff who are engaged in preparing environmentally sensitive projects usually, but not always, receive copies. The environmental "quality" of project briefs is less important than their capacity to alert those in the Bank who are particularly concerned about environmental questions. The crucial factor, once again, is the importance of an opportunity to make formal and informal contributions at the earliest possible stage in project development—well before the lines of a project are fixed.

Project preparation, like project identification, is theoretically the responsibility of the borrower but with most IDA countries, and with some others, the Bank takes the leading role. It always involves its own personnel, supplemented with consultants hired to carry out feasibility and other kinds of studies. These consultants may or may not be sensitive to environmental considerations. It was impossible to know, although several officers that were interviewed claimed that the environmental performance of the Bank's consultants was not only improving, but is often excellent enough to pull up the whole level of sensitivity to certain resource problems.

Not surprisingly, environmental awareness—or at least the degree to which action is taken on such awareness—is higher among members of the Project Advisory Staff dealing with the technical sides of projects than among the staff of the regional offices, who have the major responsibility for hurrying projects through the preparatory stage to final approval.

One aspect of project preparation deserves special attention: the examination of siting of major projects. The project preparatory process in all the development banks reviewed has been deficient in this area. All too often the environment is molded to fit preconceived plans rather than plans to fit the environment. Studies designed to gather baseline data are needed so that the dynamic interaction of project and site can be understood. These data, when coupled with regular monitoring, can explain why a project does not perform according to expectation. In conjunction with the costs and benefits associated with the noted changes, economic estimates of environmental changes associated with development can be made. These data serve to reduce uncertainty and so save money in both the long and short run. In interviews, references to baseline data were often equated with detailed biological and ecological studies that could hold up a siting decision for years. Practice has shown, however, that in the great majority of cases, sufficient baseline data for a good siting decision is already on hand if the right ecological or other environmental expertise is mobilized to locate and interpret it.

Project Appraisal

Project appraisal begins after the feasibility studies are completed. At this point the final siting for the project is determined, taking into consideration all the technical studies. If there are serious doubts about any technical, administrative, commercial, economic, or financial aspect, final approval is delayed while the preparation is redone. The project may be abandoned altogether. Environmental issues are inevitably mixed into economic and technical studies, and thus often get overlooked. Project reviewers can easily pick out faulty aspects of commercial analysis because all the data are self-contained, but cannot do so with environmental problems. External costs, such as changes in human health conditions, in habitat conditions for wildlife, and other changes in the environment, are difficult to forecast and quantify, and thus to include in the cost/benefit analysis. This problem is compounded by the fact that the Bank generally does not gather environmental information and hence has no easy basis for taking environmental changes into account. The staff is well aware of these problems and is coming up with refinements and novel solutions. However, at present, various appraisal documents do not formally consider environmental problems, although in a growing number of cases they do discuss many of these factors. For example, appraisal documents on Indonesian colonization projects contain valuable insights into the nature of the environmental constraints faced.

Any proposal for separate environmental impact statements on the U.S. model would not be appropriate, nor would it be well received. However, the more serious environmental implications of a project should be specifically identified and addressed. These problems are economic as frequently as they are technical but, unfortunately, the Bank has defined environmental evaluation as a subsidiary element of technical evaluation. The environmental integrity of an irrigation system, for example, determines its useful life and therefore limits its actual economic return. Environmental costs and benefits need to be more systematically included in cost/benefit analysis. Where this is impossible because of quantification problems, the limits of cost/benefit analysis need to be recognized and compensated for by a broader project appraisal methodology. For example, the Bank is beginning to evaluate the costs that will be incurred by a borrower if a particular project is not undertaken.

How could the environmental aspects of the appraisal process be improved? One way would be to make ecological feasibility a separate test in the appraisal process. A project would not be ecologically feasible if the interaction of man, plants, wildlife, climate, and soils were such that a necessary life-sustaining function would be critically disrupted, or if the total costs generated by the project would exceed the anticipated benefits. Using this standard would have the advantage that all environmentally related material would be self-contained, making it more comprehensive and easier to review. The costs and benefits associated with environmental changes could also be more readily determined, making it easier to plan future projects.

Throughout the World Bank, key people, particularly in the regional offices, but also on the Central Projects Staff, are too often not aware of some of the important practical environmental lessons that other parts of the Bank have learned through their successes and, more importantly, their failures. Moreover, with the growth and reorganization of the approximately 2,200 professional staff members, many people with like or critically tangential interests can no longer regularly exchange information informally. Much useful environmental experience has been committed to paper—usually short memos that could easily be circulated inside the Bank. And with a minimum of screening, much of this material could be made available not only to others in the Bank but also to other members of the development community. No one needs large volumes of paper or could find time to read it, but the Bank should make greater efforts to share—at first internally—the insights it is accumulating into environmental aspects of development.

Project Review

At this point, a project appraisal document is approved, first by the division chief (or chiefs, in the case of a project with multiple and various components), and then by department directors and the Central Project Staff. During this process, a project is submitted to OEHA for official approval—or rather the opportunity is given for official disapproval. If there are no substantive objections, the document continues up the ladder to the Loan Committee, composed of two or three senior vice presidents. Then the project is negotiated with the borrower and passed on to the board of Executive Directors for final approval. At any point along the way the project can be sent back for further work. Apparently no projects have been referred for additional environmental review by the board itself. Board members tend to be interested in broad generic issues rather than details with respect to a certain project.

Generally, by the time a project reaches the senior management level, many of the design details are immutable. It is often impossible to redesign the whole project and it may be difficult to add environmental safeguards. Therefore, in the absence of good environmental planning, the value of the senior-level reviews may be severely circumscribed. However, in all institutions under review, the pressure to keep projects on schedule is intense, so that delays imposed by high level reviews are most unwelcome. If it is known that delays are avoidable by more careful—in this instance environmentally sound—staff work, the sounder course would be more attractive.

Project Execution and Supervision

The final phase of the Bank's cycle is execution and monitoring of the designed and appraised project. The original purpose of the monitoring was to assure that the money allocated to the project was indeed spent for the project. Now, the supervisory function has been expanded. The Bank tries to use at least some of the staff associated with the appraisal of the project on its supervisory missions so that continuity is preserved. These experts represent, to the Bank's way of thinking, technical assistance in project development.

The supervisory missions which send periodic reports to the Bank regarding project execution are generally aware of environmental problems only if they have been mentioned in the appraisal report or if the effects are so large that they materially affect the outcome of the projects. Subtle or long-term changes are likely to be ignored. A management decision should be made to include comment on environmental problems, or their absence in "terms-of-reference" documents for supervisory missions, and to evaluate in supervisory reports the success of seeking solutions to these problems. In areas such as road or railroad building, or other siting problems, the manner in which a project is actually carried out means almost everything from an environmental viewpoint. These aspects should be specifically evaluated.

There have been some examples of supervisory missions finding that environmental safeguards have been ignored or bypassed. In these cases, the Bank's leverage—halting disbursements or refusing to grant loans to the country for other projects—can be used. This leverage would appear sufficient for all cases that were encountered.

Projects are also routinely subjected to formal or informal postevaluation. Depending on the project, a post-audit may occur only a few years after the end of the disbursement or many years later. If problems are identified, yet another audit may follow. Once again, however, unless environmental effects are either pronounced or mentioned in the appraisal report, it is unlikely that they will be considered by post-evaluation missions. It was surprising to discover one respect in which World Bank practice fell short in sophistication of one of the other banks studied. At the Asian Development Bank some post-audits of individual projects have been reviewed both by standards existing at the time of the project approval and by current standards. This has obvious advantages for learning purposes. The World Bank has used both techniques in a few summary reviews of programs or projects; however, so far as it was possible to ascertain, it has primarily used the first approach.

There is a growing awareness in the World Bank about the importance of evaluating, in postaudit documents, the longer-range implications and impacts, of which environmental impact is a key element. The Bank should simply be urged to go further by mandating the incorporation of such discussions—and of "current standards evaluation"—as integral parts of post-audit studies.

Conclusions

The scale and reach of the World Bank's lending, and the formidable range of its influence on the developmental and environmental practice of both borrowers and other development financing institutions, are impressive. They should not, however, divert attention from how marginal they are in relation to total development efforts being made through official aid, private foreign investment, and nationally committed resources.

The force of the Bank's leverage is limited. Despite its formidable economic strength, the Bank's environmental performance is properly bound, to a significant degree, by the priorities and proclivities of borrowing governments.

Nevertheless, in the longer run, it seems clear that the World Bank's command of a range of technical, as much as financial, expertise will increase its influence on governments' environmental outlook in relation to development planning and practice. It will grow because with increasing evidence of ecosystem fragility and the wastage of scarce resources arising from ill-planned development projects, governments will themselves come to rely on and call for better environmental planning.

The Bank's influence will also increase because, by comparison at least, it is intellectually alive and open to change while being institutionally realistic in outlook. It will also grow because, of all the multilateral development agencies, the World Bank most actively seeks to influence its borrowers to adapt development policies to a country's realities and needs. It uses dialogue with developing country governments, the financing of institution building, legal reform, training, planning, and research to help achieve these ends. Peculiarly environmental awareness in all this support work is still not very large, but the framework, and, more importantly, the will to use it, is growing.

The leadership given by the World Bank's top management on environmental development has been relatively impressive. A large part of the original impetus for incorporating environmental review into the Bank's procedures came, as was noted, from President McNamara. This is one of the factors that makes the environmental performance of the Bank outstanding when compared to other development banks. The authors of this report would only urge the desirability, articulated by Bank officers at literally every level, of the Bank's top management seeking out appropriate occasions at least one a year, by speech or in writing, to reemphasize publicly the importance attached to the integration of sound environmental thinking into every aspect of the Bank's work.

One obvious gap in expression of Bank policy is the lack of any clear and specific official linkage between lending policies to benefit the poorest, and lending to prevent the erosion or further destruction of the environments on which the poorest are so dependent but which their desperate search for a living so often threatens. This gap perhaps assumes a new significance in light of resentments increasingly expressed in many countries over emphasis on "basic needs" strategies. Making a clear linkage between help to the poorest and environmental protection may serve to remind the leadership in developing countries that to ignore or postpone help to the poorest may well undermine national security through resulting damage to national resources or to critically important ecosystems.

The importance of positive identification of environmental resource protection with good development practice can scarcely be overemphasized. Not only does it improve the chances of achieving sustainable development because it implies greater concern with protection or replacement of the resource base, but it may make an important contribution to the wider problem of public acceptance of, and support for, aid for development in general. Indeed, it is suggested that at some point the Bank's Board of Governors might consider the publicized alteration of the Bank's appellation, replacing the now anachronistic "Reconstruction" in its title with the word "Resources" to remind itself, the funders, and borrowers, that development will only occur in the future with sound management of resources both physical and natural.

Notes

1. See appendixes D, E, F, and G.

2. Reference to "World Bank" may be taken to include the International Development Association. This study did not encompass the International Finance Corporation. It is generally assumed that readers are aware of the basic structure and purposes of the World Bank Group. The Bank itself borrows through bonds floated on the world money market at commercial rates. Bank loans are based on capital raised in this way and thus must bear related rates of interest. The IDA loans made are long-term (up to fifty years) and at very low (often 2 percent) interest, with substantial grace periods.

3. World Bank Annual Report 1977, p. 9.

4. This post later became the Office of Environmental Affairs, and in 1977 became the Office of Environmental and Health Affairs (OEHA).

5. Address by Robert S. McNamara, U.N. Conference on the Human Environment, June 8, 1972. Quoted with permission.

6. See "International Environmental Concern: Impact on the Less Developed States," by Lawrence Juda (Paper presented at the Annual Meeting of the International Studies Association, St. Louis, Missouri, March, 1977).

7. Hereinafter called Environmental Handbook in text.

8. *Environmental, Health and Human Ecologic Considerations in Economic Development Projects*, World Bank, May 1974, p. 888.

9. See "World Bank Group Committed to Protecting Environments of Underdeveloped Countries," in *Environment Reporter*, vol. 8, no. 16, (August 19, 1977):615.

3

The Regional Banks

The regional banks, whose environmentally related procedures and practices we review here, vary greatly in size, in operating experience, and even to some extent in objectives. Their varied character naturally reflects the differing development priorities of their regional member states. But they share, nevertheless, similarities that invite comparison. None of them has a formally stated official position or policy on the environment; none has any staff or office with continuous and specific environmental responsibility. On the other hand, each of these banks, with the exception of the Arab Bank for Economic Development of Africa (BADEA) and the European Development Fund (EDF), which is a hybrid creature, that is, part development bank, part technical assistance agency, and thus in a sense belongs in a category of its own, has a similar set of procedures for loan evaluation, appraisal, and surveillance, generally modeled on the original example of the World Bank. Each, again excepting BADEA, which is still at an early stage of evolution institutionally, makes more or less frequent use of some form of environmental expertise over a variety of projects, though on an ad hoc basis.

Some background information on these banks is set forth so that subsequent discussion of their handling of environmental issues may be seen in the context of their range and scale of lending activities. Further data regarding the banks' membership and scale and direction of their operations is contained in appendices C, D, E, F, and G.

The Inter-American Development Bank

The Inter-American Development Bank (IDB) began its lending operations in 1961. At that time, its initial resources were on the order of $1.3 billion. One decade later, the IDB had assets of $5.5 billion, over $4 billion worth of loans had been approved, and more than $2 billion disbursed. The IDB's total paid up capital was $11.5 billion in early 1975, consisting of nearly $6 billion in ordinary capital, almost $4 billion in the Fund for Special Operations, and over $1 billion in other trust funds administered by the IDB.

The Fund for Special Operations broadly equates to the International Development Association (IDA) facility in the World Bank; since 1972 loans from these funds have been explicitly concentrated on the poorest countries of the region. IDB's special trust funds vary in purpose and size, from one of $500 million established by the Venezuelan government to finance large-scale natural resource projects to others contributed by eight countries for particular categories of social projects to be administered by the IDB under conditions agreed with the donor country.

By the end of 1976, the last year for which figures were available at the time of writing, IDB assets had climbed to almost $14.4 billion, loans totaling more than $10 billion had been approved, and some $5.8 billion had been disbursed.[1]

Unlike the World Bank (International Finance Corporation (IFC) excluded), the IDB is not limited to lending to governments, but may lend directly to government offices and, with government approval, to institutions and private enterprise of borrower countries as local intermediaries.

The IDB's approach is to inform governments that it is prepared to consider a particular loan, for which preparation could usefully be undertaken by the government. (A commitment is not made formally at this stage.) The IDB reasons that without this encouragement, governments face the awkward situation of having to reorganize, redirect, or strengthen institutions, make promises to the beneficiaries, and perhaps most importantly, authorize scarce funds for the project without all the resources to carry it out. This process of mobilization becomes simpler when the government knows that a bank programming mission has singled out the project for attention.

It is interesting to note that, in contrast to the World Bank's experience of shifting out of "productive" lending into "social improvement" lending to better to meet the needs of the poor, the IDB has never officially adopted a strategy of lending to meet "basic needs," and has been devoting an increasing share of its funds to infrastructure and mining while the relative importance of social project lending has declined. But while the IDB is moving out of social lending to some degree, it still devotes a greater percentage of its funds to these projects than the World Bank. In part, the changes in percentage of funds committed in each sector reflect a central problem that the IDB has experienced in lending its money. With a limited staff in relation to rapidly growing financial resources, the IDB has chosen to concentrate on a limited number of large-scale projects.

Pressure to approve projects and loan money could be partially responsible for the uneven concern shown in the past by the IDB over the environmental impact of its lending, although another important factor which influences the IDB's handling of environmental questions is that IDB policies are heavily influenced by its Latin American member states.[2] These governments, with a few notable exceptions, until quite recently have been extremely wary of environmental issues. In some governmental quarters, environmentalism and increasing concentration of lending on basic needs projects is still associated with a neocolonialist strategy that will slow the pace of Latin American economic development. Environmental institutions and safeguards have therefore been lax or nonexistent in Latin America. Distinct signs may now be detected, however, of changing Latin American attitudes toward environmentalism, and it is likely that the IDB's current efforts to incorporate environmental protection and enhancement more systematically into the lending process will not be ill-received by recipient governments. The third reason explaining the IDB's postponement of environmental questions has been, quite simply, the absence of a high level mandate from its president or board that it must do so.

The Asian Development Bank

The Asian Development Bank (AsDB), a considerably younger institution than the IDB, started operations only in 1966. Modeled closely on the IDB, in size the AsDB falls between the IDB and the regional banks of the African continent and the Caribbean.[3]

After a somewhat hesitant start, during which few loans were approved and the AsDB concentrated on building up a reputation for financial soundness, its activities have grown to be of considerable importance in its region. By 1973 it was funding more than 50 percent of all the multilateral capital aid projects in the region (excluding India, which has agreed not to draw on the AsDB's funds). As of 31 December 1977, a total of $4,246 million in 333 loans had been made, consisting of $3,079 million from ordinary capital and $1,167 million from special funds.

Depending on a country's anticipated ability to service the loan, together with its general economic condition, a decision is made to use ordinary capital or "softer" loans available from the special funds. As a rule, countries with a per capita income of more than $380 (1975 equivalent) will not be eligible for concessional loans. The AsDB may, however, provide blended loans from both types of resources—on a project or country basis—allowing greater help to be given to the poorer countries in line with the AsDB's charter, which provides for "special regard for the needs of smaller or less developed member countries in the region."

The AsDB also operates a technical assistance program which covers assistance in project preparation, sectoral studies, policy formulation, development planning, institution building, and so forth.

The AsDB faces similar disbursement problems to those of the IDB: a shortage of staff relative to resources and pressure to hasten its rate of disbursement. However, the International Institute for Environment and Development (IIED) team was repeatedly told that, "where appropriate," the environmental impact of projects is considered. The AsDB has been encouraged to consider the environment in its region by a general awareness of the particular environmental fragility of many parts of Asia in the face of the immense annual increase in human populations. Already the population of the inner islands of Indonesia, for example, has reached and in some cases overwhelmed the carrying capacity of local ecosystems. Bangladesh, with 30 to 70 percent of its territory inundated during the flood season, and Nepal, facing extraordinary problems of deforestation and soil erosion, make it incumbent on the AsDB to be particularly aware of potential developmental threats to the environment.

The Caribbean Development Bank

The scale of lending of the Caribbean Development Bank (CDB) is at least an order of magnitude below that of the IDB or the AsDb. Given the capital absorption capacity of the Caribbean islands, and their very modest financial resources, the CDB has concentrated on small loans. The large discrepancy between the number of loans approved and the amount disbursed is accounted for by the CDB's policy, modeled upon that of the IDB, of approving loans "in principle ' before final approval and negotiation have taken place.

Two factors combine to make the CDB of more interest from the environmental point of view than its size and level of activity alone would suggest. First, there are several influences at work in the Caribbean area that encourage environmental awareness. Chief among these is the fragility of island ecosystems which sustain a large and still growing tourist industry. Soil erosion and water supply problems, particularly, are so well known that they are almost always considered in preparatory documents for loans. Second, the CDB is a young and flexible institution and it deals with governments that have few other sources of funding. The IIED team encountered very little of the defensive posture at the CDB that was found elsewhere.

In interviews at the CDB, Bank staff emphasized the idea that because the CDB only engages in relatively small projects, the environmental impact of those projects is also necessarily small. At the same time, they claimed that with tourism the major growth industry in the region, "environment is everything." A certain failure of logic seems evident here. If the ecosystems of these islands are indeed small and fragile, a small project could result in a major disruption. There is, indeed, all the more need for environmental concern in project lending in such circumstances.

The African Development Bank

The African Development Bank (ADB), established in 1964, is unique among the regional banks in that throughout its early history the Bank was a purely regional institution without financial support from outside. The ADB was thus only able to play a very minor economic role in its early years. By 1968, of the authorized capital of 250 million ADB Units of Account (UAs)[4] only about 52 million had actually been received. This lack of resources continued until 1973, when the African Development Fund (ADF) was set up with developed country participation and an initial subscription of 77 million UA's, with 50 percent of the stock being under ADB control and the rest held by thirteen nonregional countries.

As the ADB's soft loan facility, the ADF has grown so that by the end of 1976 total loan commitments amounted to 196 million Fund Units of Account,[5] following two replenishments of the fund. A further contribution was made to the capital resources of the African Development Bank (35 million ADB UA's) following the Afro-Arab Summit of February 1977. The function of the ADF, as the soft loan facility of the ADB, parallels that of the IDA in the World Bank Group. A characteristic of both ADB and ADF lending is the large share of resources devoted to urban-related infrastructure projects.

Because of the small scale of its resources compared to other development funding institutions, the ADB, which in its early years undertook the complete financing of small- to medium-scale development projects ($3 million to $10 million), increasingly finds itself in the position of the junior partner with other regional banks (for example, the Arab development banks) or with the World Bank in its larger loans, though it remains an independent lender in the case of a large number of smaller loans. Its small size is, of course, a major factor in relation to environmental appraisal. In the case of the only project appraisal report examined which included specific environmental studies (an industrial project in West Africa), the ADB was a lending partner with the World Bank and the environmental standards were required to meet World Bank criteria. However, the ADB can claim a catalytic role in a number of loan consortia where, with a small stake of its own, it has attached substantial funding to a project prepared and appraised by it.

The Arab Bank for Economic Development of Africa

The IIED team was specifically requested by the study's sponsors to include the Arab Bank for Economic Development of Africa (BADEA) in the group of regional banks to be assessed for their environmental policies and procedures. BADEA, established in 1975, was not the most obvious of the multilateral Arab financial institutions to be studied. It is relatively small in capitalization compared to some of the other Arab banks and more constricted in geographic areas of concern.

Bilateral Arab funds such as the Kuwait Fund for Arab Economic Development (created in 1961), the Abu Dhabi Fund (1971), and the Saudi Development Fund (1974) preceded BADEA, as did the Arab Fund for Economic and Social Development, established in Kuwait in 1968, the Islamic Development Bank (1974), the Organization of Arab Petroleum Exporting Countries' (OAPEC) Special Fund (1974), the Special Arab Fund for Africa, and the Fund for Arab African Technical Assistance (1973).[6] Certainly, at least some of these institutions deserve review, and their approaches to the environment should be examined. However, BADEA is of particular interest in the context of the present report in that it is the only development financing institution studied that is controlled and financed solely by a group of Third World countries. BADEA also plays a significant role as a coordinator of other multilateral and bilateral Arab financial institutions.

With a subscribed capital of $231 million in 1975, an additional pledge of $544 million to be added to this base in 1978, and only eleven professionals in its Operations Department in mid-1977, BADEA had lent, from its inception to mid-1977, over $186 million. But it clearly has not so far been able to complete a full project cycle from project identification through to detailed appraisal. In fact, a critically important policy position adopted by the Bank from the point of view of environmental assessment was its decision to devote few of BADEA's resources to feasibility studies and identification of projects. BADEA's officials claim that a great volume of preinvestment studies exist "on the shelf" in the case of most African countries.

The Regional Banks' Environmental Procedures and Practice

None of the regional banks that were examined, and indeed, neither of the technical assistance agencies studied has a formal office or division for environmental matters with responsibility for project review or surveillance. However, as this section will reveal, the situation is a fast-changing one, and there is a substantial amount of environmental study and analysis conducted on an ad hoc project-by-project basis.

In the case of the Inter-American Development Bank (IDB), there is strong evidence of recently heightened environmental awareness. This has undoubtedly been occasioned in part by the fact that it has its headquarters in Washington, D.C., which allows for close contacts with the World Bank and the U.S. Congress.[7]

The Inter-American Development Bank: Procedures and Practice

Although interviews uncovered a recognition of the need for environmental planning in the development process, the Inter-American Development Bank to date has not formally announced an overall policy or procedures for including environmental factors in the loan process. Guidelines outlining environmental considerations in certain sectors were approved at the departmental level four years ago, but were not integrated into the published sector guidelines used and distributed for project formulation until late last year, when revised guidelines were issued for electric energy and agricultural development. (See chapter 8.) In some sectors the IDB has established procedures without openly formulating a clear policy. For example, an informal Bank document states that "before considering an energy project for financing, the Bank requires the applicant to submit an environmental impact statement as part of the technical-economic feasibility report to support its loan request."

The absence of a top-level commitment, despite the fact that various documents have been circulating within the IDB for several years, has meant that environmental assessment rarely reaches down to the country review level. Depending on the state of development of the prospective borrowing country, the Bank may be quite materially involved in identification and feasibility studies. Particularly in the poorer countries, the more the IDB is involved in loan preparation, the greater should be the opportunity to incorporate environmental factors.

Some loan officers and officials in the IDB accept that the environmental impacts of development are important, and are concerned that these impacts not be limited to the narrow focus of pollution control. But it was more difficult to locate staff with the broader environmental sensitivity needed to discuss the converse proposition that development itself is restrained by environmental degradation and abuse of natural resources. For example, in the past several years concern has been shown in the United Nations Development Programme, the United Nations Environment Programme (UNEP), the Organization of American States (OAS), the World Bank, and elsewhere that rural energy needs cannot be met in Latin America by traditional forms of power sector lending, even in light of a growing commitment to rural electrification. (See chapter 7.) The IDB's contribution to this gestation of ideas and action has been minimal, with the exception of its extensive rural electrification program. The view that aid institutions should not duplicate one another's work certainly merits careful consideration. But the IDB is such a critical institution for the development effort of many Latin American countries that it can hardly afford not to emphasize an area of concern as significant as the basic energy needs of the large percentage of Latin America's population, who will not be served for the foreseeable future by centrally generated power supplies.[8]

The present situation is, as noted, in a state of flux. A draft environmental policy paper has been prepared for review by departmental managers and will be presented to the IDB Board in 1978. This paper results from an intensive internal review and external consultative process which was headed by a senior bank official. In addition, at the time of this study, a consultant working at the IDB was developing environmental checklists for field and headquarters staff in the transport sector. Future plans call for sectoral checklists in the areas of electric power, irrigation, fisheries, agricultural development, urbanization, forestry, water and sewage, and industrial projects. The new environmental sector guidelines are meant to consider ways of helping recipient countries to develop their own environmental policy in a given area. This appears to be a welcome and badly needed innovation.

For several reasons, there seems to be little possibility that an environmental office along the lines of the World Bank's Office of Environmental and Health Affairs (OEHA) will be recommended. Considerable resistance exists within the IDB to the creation of such an office, which is seen by some staff as threatening to apply a brake to project preparation. There is also the already mentioned lingering reluctance to elaborate environmental concerns, both within the IDB and in its member countries. A central office might be effective within the Bank, but some IDB staff believe that it would be too isolated to achieve the Bank's paramount goal of helping governments plan environmentally acceptable projects.

Environmental considerations will remain submerged at the IDB unless there is some focal point with the responsibility and authority to raise environmental issues and give them visibility. It should be established at the outset that environmental review is needed at the earliest possible stage of project identification, and not at a stage when redirection or adaptation of the project is impossible without major delays. Also, it should not be overlooked that environmental review of projects creates considerable pressure on staff to whom that responsibility falls, so much so that individuals who are assigned review responsibilities might not have time to work on the equally important assignment of raising environmental awareness among the IDB's staff at large. Perhaps that important task should be explicitly singled out and delegated.

The choice of whether to establish a formal environmental review office, at the IDB or elsewhere, is not a clear one. There are risks associated with not isolating clear responsibility for environmental review. As discussed in chapter 2, the surest compensation for these risks may be to establish environmental or ecological feasibility as one of the standard tests of project appraisal. Thus, a board of directors (at the IDB or elsewhere) would not simply assume that the environment has been considered by an environmentally aware staff, but would be able to review and question that element of project appraisal and would thereby be able to monitor the implementation of its policy directives, just as it can monitor the implementation of economic, managerial, and other policies.

Early "environmental intelligence" at the stage of project identification, using environmental expertise working with the IDB's substantive staff in the field, who in turn work with ministries on project preparation, could be a key component in incorporating environmental considerations into the basic design of loan proposals. The IDB's relatively decentralized structure could be an advantage here, particularly since the staff seem committed to encouraging the active support and cooperation of member governments for any environmental assessment procedures which are eventually established. This seems important since in many cases the field staffs may come under heavier political influence than an operation working in Washington.

The IDB views certain types of projects as environmental protection projects per se, for example sewer systems or water supply projects. For these types of projects, the Bank has begun to bring in environmental consultants to assure that the assistance will accomplish its objectives. There has also been a move within the IDB's Economic and Social Development Department to improve the methodology of cost/benefit analysis to include "externalities," such as quantifiable costs of transportation to work for people displaced by development projects. In this connection, an interesting recent innovation at the IDB has been the establishment of the Project Methodology Unit in the Economic and Social Development Department which has authority to pick up projects in the preparatory pipeline and to reconsider the scope and methods of project analysis.

The loan process of the IDB requires a review by the loan committee which includes the general counsel or his representative. This review is important, for the formulation of the loan contract offers an additional opportunity for inclusion of an environmental clause. (At least one member of the IDB's legal staff regularly introduces environmental clauses, but the procedure is not at present general, or even apparently common.) The loan committee should, as a matter of course, raise questions about the ways environmental considerations are being taken into account in the development of the project. Further, the committee should not hesitate to insist, on the basis that no project can proceed without its approval, that its questions be fully and satisfactorily answered.

From the foregoing it is evident that the view of the environment taken at the IDB is still largely a function of individual interest, which affects consideration of the environmental side effects of development projects, as well as direct environmental improvement. At the same time, there seems to be considerable scope within the current lending process for environmental considerations to be included in IDB's operations.

The Asian Development Bank: Procedures and Practice

The Asian Development Bank (AsDB) lacks any formal constitutional commitment to environmental protection, and it has no specific procedures or check-lists for ensuring that various aspects of environmental impact are considered in the loan preparatory process. Environmental responsibilities at the AsDB are thus left to loan officers in organizing project appraisal. Environment is not, however, seen by Bank officials as solely the responsibility of the borrower government. The IIED team was informed that "procedures, manuals, etc., for general (environmental) guidance will be developed in due course ... " But, AsDB officials made it clear that the environmental modifications which a government would accept in loan proposals were limited.

Some divisions of the AsDB (water supply and urban development, power, industry, regional development, and agricultural development) have manuals for project appraisal, but so far only a new "Manual for Water Supply Appraisal" appears to contain any specific reference to environmental considerations. It is left to the loan officer concerned to incorporate environmental considerations in the instructions for an appraisal mission. The response of several officers to questions concerning use of project manuals and formal briefing was that, in practice, briefing was usually verbal and informal—apparently a matter of discussing an original loan request and handing it over to an appraisal team.

Detailed responses by officers in interviews indicate difficulties faced by the AsDB in seeking to incorporate an environmental component into its development work, including shortage of staff and pressure of time. However, the claim was repeatedly made that "where appropriate" the environmental impact of projects is considered.

Although the AsDB has no formal procedures to check on the incorporation of environmental considerations into loan projects, Bank officials pointed to a number of projects, especially coal and hydropower, port development, fertilizer and cement plants, water supply and sewage plants, and a palm oil processing project, where specific assurances or guarantees had been obtained from the executing agency (generally a government department) that environmental controls and "standards satisfactory to the Bank" were to be applied. In the instances examined, the environmental standards insisted upon were adopted from the World Bank or from guidelines of the U.S. Agency for International Development (USAID).

Assurances from governments of project modifications to prevent environmental damage are achieved generally by covenants or agreements to "side letters." In the case of one upper-reaches river management project, for example, the IIED team was shown a side letter in which the government undertook to reforest seven thousand hectares as a precondition to the AsDB funding a flood control and irrigation project.

Discussions with senior Bank officials regarding possible improvements to current environmental practices elicited the view that problems of this kind were not best tackled by setting up separate departments and procedures but should be handled on an individual basis. In one top official's words, "knowledge of that [environmental] type should permeate all departments." Many AsDB officials took the view that specialized knowledge is not necessary to perceive the potential environmental impact or side effects of a loan project. This fact surely makes it all the more essential that adequate environmental awareness and knowledge really do permeate each department. At the same time it is questionable whether a focal point for disseminating environmental awareness and promoting more thorough environmental assessment is unnecessary.

However, the approach to these issues at the AsDB is not altogether rigid, and a certain confusion exists as to how to think about environmental problems.

Most officers interviewed spoke of environmental studies or consultancy work done on an ad hoc basis on water supply, power, and industrial projects, including one or two projects (like the Laguna de Bay project) whose primary purpose is environmental improvement of a polluted water source. No one referred unprompted, however, to environmental studies associated with regional development projects, though on further interviewing and documentary examination it became clear that this is an area of the worst environmental disasters of the Asian region, especially because of problems of forest clearance and soil erosion.

Lack of specific in-house environmental expertise seems to be part of a broader problem in the AsDB. The Bank grew very rapidly indeed in the mid-1970s, so much so that all of its divisions appeared to be under excessive workloads. The AsDB's management is currently concerned about the problem of staff overload; total professional staff numbers only about 288, even though in 1977 forty-five major loans were made totaling $887 million, a 34 percent increase over 1975. Inquiries as to whether specific environmental expertise would be added to any part of the AsDB during major forthcoming staff reorganization and expansion met with a rather negative response. It seems clear that the AsDB, whose cumulative loans now total over $4.2 billion, needs to study ways of engaging fresh environmental expertise in the loan appraisal process. It does not seem safe to assume that, given a new degree of environmental awareness, which is now present in the Bank, the same groups of technical consultants that have been used in the past will necessarily be able to make adequate environmental assessments in the future. The AsDB's response to this conclusion is that it recognizes that different kinds and degrees of environmental problems require different degrees and kinds of expertise and also different degrees of attention. The AsDB does consult various agencies such as the World Health Organization (WHO), UNEP, and so forth, and "engages experts as required and suitable for study and solving the problem." Despite this response, however, it seems clear that the need for professional and systematic environmental assessment capacity (within the house) should be studied by the AsDB as a matter of urgency.

In the last two years, management has shown a strong interest in "appropriate technology," on which an AsDB Occasional Paper was recently prepared (April 1977). AsDB interest in appropriate technology stems from the acute employment problems of Asia and the extreme shortage of capital. It seems possible that management may be willing to incorporate environmental considerations into "loan desk" thinking in a similar way, though they would only want to address themselves to "specific environmental problems identified during the planning and coordination of development projects." A broader approach may, however, be required if more environmentally sensitive solutions to development problems are to be incorporated from the outset.

The time may well be ripe for AsDB's management to consider proposals for some environmental assessment mechanism in the Bank. One of its most senior staff believed that there "was a case for some more capacity in the Bank for access to new ideas." He had in mind a "multipurpose observatory" for development and environment technologies and ideas which could "be regional and could serve development financing institutions."

Finally, with the AsDB, as elsewhere, the authors were constantly reminded of the limitations of what was acceptable to borrower countries in the way of environmental conditions, and also of the considerable additional constraint that the AsDB is only able to supply the foreign exchange component of projects. This last constraint may reinforce the penchant of governments, and of the Bank's technical advisors, for imported and capital intensive technological solutions.

The Caribbean Development Bank: Procedures and Practice

No formally agreed upon environmental policy exists at the Caribbean Development Bank (CDB) and indeed there is a marked tendency to say that there cannot be any environmental problems because the Bank does not lend to large industrial or infrastructure projects. This narrow view is somewhat balanced, however, by sound work in the agriculture department, which sees good agricultural practice as incorporating many of the characteristics that might be termed "environmental." For some time, the CDB has considered attaching a new staff member to the president's office who would be given a broad mandate to look at environmental and social implications of loans, but this idea seems to be gaining very little momentum. The CDB lacks clear environmental criteria, and has not often worked closely with governments on environmental problems. But it is committed to improvement on both fronts, and could well benefit from the addition of a new social/environmental officer, who should be able to identify gaps in expertise which could be filled by consultants. As lending grows, it will become more important to have better coordination of intersectoral programs. A glimmer of this appears in a recent environmentally sensitive paper on integrated rural development.

Many of the projects funded by the CDB, particularly housing and agriculture, require considerable management and training programs which should include an environmental component if they are to be sustained. The CDB, however, does not at present include any funds for training in its loan packages. This oversight may in fact be the Bank's critical shortcoming at present and its negative environmental effect may be as great as its possible impact on the CDB's development goals. The thoroughness of environmental assessment work seems to depend to a large degree on the interests of the individual officer. A new *Project Procedures Manual* has recently been issued, which unfortunately fails to mention environment as an aspect of project preparation or appraisal.

Insofar as including environmental expertise in program missions is concerned, it seems that little has been accomplished thus far. However, the CDB has to revise loan applications so extensively that there may be little point in presenting governments with detailed environmental considerations at this stage.

In sum, the CDB approach is presently one of ad hoc environmental considerations, which are often well taken into account, but even minimal efforts to systematize the process have so far met with no success.

The African Development Bank:
Procedures and Practice

The African Development Bank (ADB) not only lacks formal procedures for environmental assessment, but its staff generally displays limited awareness of the broader range of environmental concerns relevant to development lending.

The operational sections of the ADB/ADF are divided into the Project and Operations Departments. The Project Department deals with all technical aspects of projects. Its two divisions contain specialists in agriculture, transport, health, public utilities and telecommunications, financial analysis, and financial administration. The Operations Department handles the loan induction process and contains a division which produces economic studies of member countries. This division is regionally divided into six sections: Central Africa, North Africa, West Africa 1 and 2, East Africa, and Southern Africa. The division is staffed by economists, loan officers (including a considerable number of civil engineers), and legal advisors. It seems that it would be in this division that procedures for environmental assessment would have to be supervised and undertaken under guidance of the specialists of the Project Division. However, the ADB has carried through a major reorganization since the visit of the IIED team, so that no firm conclusions should be drawn until the procedures of the new organization have been observed.

As regards environmental practice, much the same picture appears to obtain for the ADB as for the AsDB. The principal point which emerged in discussion of loan development procedures and our attempts to establish whether any environmental assessment checks or appraisals had been introduced into the loan preparation process, was that the ADB (like BADEA) has not financed preinvestment studies, and where it has initiated them it has tended to rely on the UNDP and other agencies to carry them out. However, the ADB does provide financing for appraisal missions which are usually carried out by Bank staff, sometimes with the addition of one or two outside consultants. The ADB also provides advisory services and staff from its own resources to help countries with the development of loans. Feasibility studies regarding the viability and shape of specific projects are carried out by consultants, often financed by grants made to the Bank from various sources.

Overall, sectoral shifts in lending, especially in the ADB itself, may indicate that much greater attention is now being focused on basic needs, including rural projects, than in the earlier years of the Bank. (See appendix F.) In the case of a number of the rural development projects, the agricultural economists interviewed seemed to be quite sensitive to issues of environmental conservation.

What was more surprising, however, was that despite the African location of UNEP and the comparatively high level of environmental awareness in many parts of Africa due to the Sahelian drought, problems of soil erosion, major disease control campaigns, and so forth, attitudes encountered within ADB were not so much skeptical or hostile as uncomprehending of what the IIED team described as environmental concern.

For example, in the field of energy there was apparently a complete absence of any interest in the ADB in the possibility of studying solar, wind, or other income energy sources as applicable to African problems. This absence may be mainly the result of the past heavy bias towards large scale, urban-based, infrastructure projects (especially roads and telecommunications) which is evident from the earlier pattern of Bank lending. When questioned, Bank officials strongly emphasized the dependence of the ADB on governmental requests which favored this pattern of lending.

It also seemed apparent, although it should be emphasized that ADB contacts were limited by the absence of a number of key officials, that the Bank's project officers and technical experts appear to rely on a group of consulting engineers, agricultural economists, and so forth, whose thinking is anchored to traditional growth patterns of development. Thus, despite signs of changed thinking in the 1975 and 1976 ADB annual reports (for example, the new interest in food and energy self-sufficiency), the impression was that this change was still largely rhetorical and that the pattern of appraisal and consultancy advice remained much as before.

Environmental Assessment and the Arab Bank for
Economic Development of Africa

As is implied in the brief profile of the Arab Bank for Economic Development of Africa (BADEA) in the previous section, there are no environmental assessment procedures in the Bank. The only relevant guideline in the *Principles Governing the Bank's Policy* is that the Bank should "ensure maximum returns for the utilization of its resources" and "urge African countries, if need be, to reconsider some of their priorities." Environmental assessment as such did not figure in the thinking of the BADEA at this stage, though more than one staff member interviewed felt that this was a serious shortcoming. It was felt that the

Bank should get some help and advice on the question of environmental assessment, and it was confirmed that no environmental advisor had so far been used by BADEA. Bank staff, admittedly, were in the dark as to what the environmental dimensions of development projects might imply, and indeed their view of environment was generally restricted to water projects, desertification, and industrial pollution.

Conclusions

To summarize the findings of inquiries at five regional development banks, and taking into account the wide variation among the banks' abilities fully to manage their projects, it seems that none of these organizations has paid sufficient attention to the environmental dimension of its development program. Procedures have not been established, so that environment is only considered in a haphazard fashion, usually due to the initiative of an individual member of staff. Very few loan decisions have been seriously altered under this unguided approach. There are notable exceptions, of course, but these usually reflect particular local circumstances.

More disconcerting, however, was the discovery of a lack of perception among staff at the regional banks regarding the dependence of the development process on the environment. Policy papers, appraisal guidelines, and project preparation have generally failed to refer to this interrelationship. To the misfortune of the impoverished people whose basic needs cannot be met in existing circumstances, problems of resource depletion and environmental degradation have for the most part been overlooked.

Given the general lack of recognition that environmental factors can seriously retard development, it is hardly surprising that formal environmental assessment procedures have not been established by any of the regional banks. (The Inter-American Development Bank may soon alter this picture, as has already been discussed in some detail.) It is not by any means suggested that the first action in every bank should necessarily be the creation of a separate environmental office. It is, however, recommended that the leadership of each aid institution define its concept of necessary environmental protection standards, and the procedures needed to achieve them. Such an exercise will, however, be of little value unless at the same time an individual or organizational focal point is given responsibility to oversee and build upon this process.

It also seems clear that major changes in these institutions will only occur if a forceful policy statement is issued and responsibility assigned for its implementation. This should be based on a thorough internal review of environmental issues and their relation to each institution's development work. The unique circumstances of each institution must dictate whether an environmental review office will eventually be needed to address these problems, or whether a less formal environmental focal point should guide the process.

But beyond a strong public commitment to change, several different types of problems should be addressed by each of the institutions here covered. Specifically, any environmental initiative should be based upon consideration of two points: first, while it can be helpful to identify the exact location of environmental responsibility, it is critical not to isolate environment from the daily work of bank lending operations. Active environmental planning should permeate both the identification and preparation phases of a project, rather than be left to the formal appraisal phase when basic design and siting are extremely difficult to reconsider. There is the danger that an overworked environmental officer would be left to detect obvious environmental abuses rather than to influence the larger patterns and practices of operations. This danger leads to the second critical function that must be performed very soon, namely to take active measures to raise environmental awareness and expertise among the operational staff. This may entail modification of existing staff training patterns to include an environmental dimension. At the very least, every project or loan officer needs to be able to recognize those situations which require further environmental expertise, perhaps in the form of a consultant. One possibly useful way to come to agreement on exactly what aspects of environmental practice should be emphasized may be to get project officers to prepare lists of key environmental problems in their own areas of cognizance. This same material could form the basis of eventual guideline documents.

It seems, then, that each regional institution should assess how its own circumstances dictate that these issues be addressed at the earliest opportunity. In some areas UNEP or such organizations as the Food and Agriculture Organization (FAO) should probably play a more active role, particularly in Africa, where there has been a proliferation of development financing institutions. In most cases great benefit, it seems, could be received from closer liaison with the World Bank which has expressed its willingness to share the lessons of its eight years' experience.

Notes

1. Inter-American Development Bank, *Annual Report*, 1976, pp. vi-vii and 28-29.
2. Canada, Japan, the United States, Yugoslavia, and certain Western European countries are important sources of financing for the IDB; however, the regional member states seem to exert greater influence on overall policy-making than occurs at some other regional institutions. The IDB is acutely aware of member government priorities.
3. See appendix G for a description of the AsDB project cycle.
4. ADB Units of Account (ADB UA 1 = US $1.20).
5. Fund Units of Account (FUA 1 = US $1.11).

6. In 1977 this fund (SAAFA) was merged with **BADEA**.

7. For example, in congressional hearings, Representative David Obey raised questions regarding how the IDB dealt with environmental questions, the procedures established and implemented, and the projects changed or turned down because of environmental problems. See *Foreign Assistance and Related Agencies Appropriations for 1978*. Hearings Before a Subcommittee of the Committee on Appropriations, U.S. House of Representatives, 95th Congress, First Session, Part 1, p. 521.

8. For a much fuller discussion of these issues and of the directions IDB energy lending may next take, see chapter 7.

4 United Nations Development Programme and the Organization of American States

The United Nations Development Programme (UNDP) and the Organization of American States (OAS) are largely different from the other institutions included in this study since the development assistance they provide is all made in the form of grants, not loans. The OAS is basically a political organization, but it has economic, scientific, and training functions that are relevant to this study. The UNDP is a development organization that supports a very wide range of technical assistance, research, and preinvestment endeavors. Both organizations depend on voluntary contributions from member states for the bulk of their resources, which in turn determine their scale of activities. The UNDP has found itself, for a variety of reasons, in a state of continual reconsideration of its purposes and functions. Reorganizations and reorientations have made its job more difficult than it would otherwise have been. The OAS, in contrast, seems to be one of the world's more stable intergovernmental organizations, and works closely with its member governments to help coordinate various activities.

The Organization of American States

The Office of the Secretary General of the OAS is composed of four major subdivisions, of which two have environmentally related functions: the Executive Secretariat for Economic and Social Affairs, and the Executive Secretariat for Educational, Scientific and Cultural Affairs. These two subsecretariats respond to requests for technical assistance, training, and institutional development from the member countries, and in addition, may act as executing entities for projects of nonmember governments and other international organizations such as the UNDP.

The Program of Regional Development (PRD), a subdivision of the Secretariat for Economic and Social Affairs, provides help to member states in four principal fields: (1) evaluation of the natural resources of regions and river basins; (2) integrated regional development planning based on social, economic, spatial, and environmental criteria; (3) the formulation and evaluation of specific development projects; and (4) environmental management planning. It has an annual budget of approximately $2.5 million which is more or less matched by the member states' "counterpart" funds for individual projects. Additional funds on the order of $1 to 2 million are sometimes also handled by the PRD in its capacity of executing or contract agency.

With an annual budget of about $10 million, the Regional Scientific and Technological Development Program builds up indigenous research capability, particularly of Latin American universities and research institutions; it tries to guide and coordinate national research programs; and, in a few special projects, it tries to find practical applications for innovative technology in critical areas. Within the Department of Scientific Affairs, the Basic Sciences Unit supports governmental ability to conduct scientific studies, including ecological surveys. Roughly $400,000 is spent annually on environmental and conservation work. The Applied Sciences Unit spends $2.5-3.0 million annually on practical research, including alternative energy and marine and water pollution work.

The United Nations Development Programme

In 1976, UNDP committed $430 million to new preinvestment studies and technical assistance services. The First Programming Cycle (for the period 1972-1976) saw UNDP meet its target of $1,538 million in assistance delivered. Overall, the UNDP is supporting 45 percent of a program of preinvestment projects which on completion will have cost $5,000 million. In view of the scale of operations in which UNDP participates, and the multiplier effect of its preinvestment resource surveying and feasibility work, as well as its planning support and training activities, it might be argued that UNDP activities could have an importance in relation to the environmental soundness of development-funded projects greater than that of any institution included in this study, with the possible exception of the World Bank.

In order to shift more forcefully toward the strategy of meeting the needs of the poorest, the UNDP anticipates that its Second Programming Cycle:

> will see considerably increased emphasis by governments on two classes of projects. In the first class will be those related to problems of reshaping international economic relationships—trade and tariff negotiations, commodity pricing and marketing, redressing some of the current imbalance in industrial and technological capacity, and orienting private investment more closely with development goals. The second category will involve activities designed for greatest possible impact at the grass-roots—improving nutrition, increasing employment and earnings, safeguarding health, expanding education, up-grading housing and strengthening social services.[1]

Because of UNDP's decentralized nature and the autonomy enjoyed by the specialized agencies that execute the great bulk of UNDP projects in project preparation, responsibility for environmental planning is difficult to locate. The UNDP rarely acts alone or has undisputed control over a project. In a paper submitted to the governing council in 1977, the administrator gave his view of the tangled relationship:

There is hardly any facet of its role or activities to which UNDP can do justice without the fullest support and co-operation of its partner agencies. The Administrator therefore holds the conviction that UNDP must and can exercise its responsibilities in a way which enhances the important functions of the Specialised Agencies, and which in no way preempts or duplicates their efforts.[2]

Clearly this must be the administrator's view, as it is the official policy of the United Nations. But it can hardly facilitate the task of environmental assessment of UNDP-supported projects in practice, since the "substantive" responsibility for these frequently falls to a specialized agency. However, an interagency task force has been organized to coordinate the work of UNDP and the executing agencies, and this might be the appropriate forum for coordinating an approach to environmental implications of projects. It has been agreed, perhaps unfortunately, that the United Nations Environment Programme (UNEP) need not be a full time working member of this task force, but a UNEP representative will be invited when needed. It would be unfortunate if the arrangement were to imply an assumption that UNEP must bear environmental responsibilities when they arise in place of sound environmental practice by UNDP and the agencies themselves.

The UNDP's country programming procedure is designed to enable governments to choose in advance those areas where they can count on UNDP help. It is negotiated by a resident representative. When one considers the relative autonomy of the UNDP's executing agencies United Nations Educational, Scientific and Cultural Organization (UNESCO), the World Health Organization (WHO), the Food and Agriculture Organization (FAO), and so forth, and the degree to which many governments rely on their technical advice, and when one considers the special relationships and the sectoral ministries of governments, it becomes clear that the potential role of the UNDP resident representative's office as a focal point for overall environmental assessment is generally very limited. All too frequently the overview of environmental impacts falls to people who are unwilling or unable to take a broad integral and long-term view of project design, which is so often essential for sound environmental planning.

This division of planning responsibility is a fact of political life for UNDP. The UNDP does not, however, absolve itself from qualitative responsibility for country programmes and the resulting projects:

The content of country programmes will continue to be determined by each Government. The fundamental respect for national sovereignty which is the cornerstone of UNDP's philosophy, however, in no way *absolves* UNDP and its partner agencies from *responsibility* for the appropriateness of the technical co-operation provided and the way in which the particular development objective is sought: the mandate to ensure that technical cooperation spurs development. Thus, while Governments have an inalienable right to decide what they want to achieve with UNDP assistance, the UN system has an inescapable responsibility to advise on how those objectives might be attained, as an intrinsic part of the whole function of technical co-operation.[3] [Emphasis added.]

The country programming procedure could perhaps be adapted to different uses, but at present it does not serve as an economic or social planning mechanism. The UNDP in particular stresses the importance of flexibility to facilitate response to the short-term wishes of governments. Such wishes rarely reflect, and may be inconsistent with, environmentally sound development planning.

Environmental Procedures and Practices

The Organization of American States:
Procedures and Practice

Environment is not a subject on which the Organization of American States (OAS) has overall policies, although as an organization it appears to have a strong interest in the environment and certainly sponsors a number of environmental activities. An example of its environmental interest was the formation of an Inter-Secretarial Committee on the Human Environment which was primarily responsible for coordinating OAS activities in worldwide meetings such as the Stockholm, Habitat, Desertification, and World Water Conferences.

In 1975, the Program of Regional Development (PRD) allocated a staff position to environmental protection. The incumbent participates as a member of the field team in some technical assistance projects, and in all cases provides technical advisory services. He also participates in the PRD policy committee.

Until recently, there was very little the PRD could do to improve project requests that omitted any reference to the environment. However, terms of reference for negotiating an environmental objective are now being provided to appraisal mission teams who develop requests for technical assistance into detailed work plans that later become the basis for agreements between the OAS and the government. If applied with perseverance, this innovation could induce significant changes in the attitudes of OAS member governments.

In order to include environmental guidelines in contract agreements, an element of PRD's strategy is to build on local laws (such as management and use of land and natural resources, social development, and health protection laws) which provide a legal basis for the incorporation of environmental considerations into development planning. For example, a Peruvian water law authorizes the government to formulate policies for water use and development and to plan and administer its conservation, preservation, and rational use. The PRD could perhaps use such a law to formulate environmental guidelines for explicit inclusion in contract agreements.

The OAS claims that responses to its initiatives have been positive in that environmental quality objectives are now almost routinely included in technical assistance missions at the reconnaissance and prefeasibility planning level, and all regional development planning courses and seminars given by the training centers connected with the PRD include a unit on environmental protection.

The OAS has also had some success coordinating the environmental activities of its different branches. For example, the PRD has assembled proposals that incorporate an environmental dimension into plans for the far headwater regions (deserts and swamp) of the Plata River.[4] Meanwhile, the Applied Sciences Unit of the Department of Scientific Affairs has undertaken estuarial studies, including an evaluation of discharge effects on the nearby ocean. As a result, a remarkably complete set of baseline data is being gathered on the full effects of dam construction.[5]

There are, however, important areas of member state activities about which the OAS has not been consulted or even kept officially informed. In the area of human settlements, the OAS has had little, if any, role in project formulation for metropolitan areas. In rural development, the impact on environmental considerations seems to have been limited to proposing action on extreme soil erosion, an activity in which the PRD appears to have been outstandingly effective.

The OAS's dependence on national requests continues to severely limit its initiating role. The PRD cannot go directly to development banks with project proposals, but must wait for a member government to submit a project before contacting financing agencies. This results in long delays, and comprehensive plans or interrelated sets of recommendations tend to disintegrate. The difficulties experienced by governments in getting on with comprehensive, integrated programs reinforce this tendency.

The United Nations Development Programme:
Procedures and Practice

UNDP management has a general awareness of environmental problems, but takes the view that these should be the concern of both UNEP and whichever institution carries out the project which UNDP funds. Various official UNDP documents and manuals mention environment as one among a number of considerations which those who devise projects might be advised to consider in particular circumstances. Beginning in 1973, a number of "Technical Advisory Notes" were prepared to inform personnel on the right technical questions to raise about different types of projects in each economic and social sector. Several notes mention environmental considerations. Finally, one staff member in UNDP's small Technical Advisory Division (TAD) has been requested, along with his other responsibilities, to keep up-to-date and informed about environmental matters and to be primarily responsible for handling requests for information relating to UNDP and the environment.

Project responsibility in UNDP falls to the regional bureaus at headquarters in New York, which sometimes seek advice from the TAD. Frequently, however, projects are developed and supervised by regional staff without regard to the available technical expertise, and TAD personnel have far too much work to find time to troubleshoot on their own initiative.

Within the TAD, environmental considerations may be included on an ad hoc basis as part of a long list of technical aspects of the project to be reviewed. However, concern with the environmental soundness of projects remains a rather peripheral consideration in relation to the UNDP's developmental focus. With no systematic monitoring to assess whether or not the instructions and guidelines are in fact being followed, and no measures to require compliance with them, it may be concluded that the effectiveness of these procedures is minimal.

At the country level, UNDP does conduct reviews of current and future programs, but here again environmental considerations are not specifically taken into account. Under UNDP's decentralized operations the Resident Representatives have power in a number of spheres both for recommending projects and for approving, on the spot, projects of less than $400,000. They are *not* required to take any formal or procedural note of environmental aspects in projects under consideration, although UNEP has in some instances held briefings for them and has communicated its interest in several categories of projects with serious environmental implications.[6]

One hopeful sign, if it is not lost in the bureaucratic maze that so frequently engulfs these initiatives, is the establishment of an Evaluation Programme or management plan, by the Bureau for Policy Planning. The management plan, among other purposes, is intended to create an "institutional memory" and to focus priorities on various sectors. Staff are currently so overwhelmed by operational responsibilities, particularly in the TAD, that no one has time for reflective analysis of notably successful or unsuccessful projects.

If this Programme could operate successfully, it should be a particularly useful mechanism for learning from past environmental mistakes. However, the 1978-1979 draft Programme included nineteen subject areas for evaluation, but excluded environment. A senior UNDP official agreed that environmental planning, given its inherently long-range character, could be uniquely served by this process. It should, without question, be included in the next Evaluation Programme. This seems particularly urgent when one recalls that prevention of environmental degradation is so often intimately related to meeting basic human needs, which is one of the two declared foci of UNDP's Second Programming Cycle.

In 1973, the UNDP set up an ill-fated and recently abandoned Task Force on the Human Environment located in the Industry, Housing and Technology Division of the UN's Regional Commission for Asia and the Pacific (ESCAP). It was conceived as an experiment to support and facilitate the work of UNDP's local offices. In practice, however, the Task Force met considerable difficulty in its efforts to visit ten member governments. These governments had signed the Task Force Project Document and had agreed, in principle at least, to accept visits from teams designed to identify for development planners what their own governments' environmental agencies, offices, or commissions were trying to do. The Task Force was also greatly reduced in effectiveness by the UNDP financial cutbacks of 1975-1976 when its originally proposed five- or six-man team was cut to two.

Aside from the work of the Task Force, UNDP has not taken any significant general initiative in encouraging governments to consider environmental factors in their project formulation. In some instances, however, UNDP has indicated that environmental considerations needed further review by the government and has managed to rectify a faulty project. UNDP staff were pleased, for example, with the encouragement they had given to further ecological study of the proposed Jonglei Canal in the Sudan.

UNDP does support a number of projects of a specifically environmental nature. It has, for example, supported environmental sanitation feasibility studies and pollution control research; it has funded a range of projects aimed at beneficial environmental modification including pollution control, irrigation and flood control, and estuarine control. (See chapter 8.) Many of these projects are subsequently financed by a regional development bank. In addition, the public health projects which UNDP funds, such as the program in a multi-nation area in West Africa for the removal of onchocerciasis, may be considered environmental improvement projects. The record, therefore, is one of substantial involvement in many aspects of environmental impact amelioration.

It may be argued that UNDP's decentralized approach is the best way of avoiding the rigidities of specific standardized environmental criteria and adapting environmental considerations so that they are optimally acceptable to governments. However, the inclusion of greater ecological and biological expertise in the UNDP headquarters Technical Advisory Division could bring needed expertise into the project review process while helping the Regional Bureaus at UNDP headquarters to offset the sometimes excessively narrow and specialized formulation of projects permitted by the sectoral Specialized Agencies. (However, in some areas such as forestry, there is already good cooperation.)

In summary, UNDP's record in environmental planning and protection has not been impressive. In fairness, though, it labors under handicaps not suffered by any other institution included in this study. It is probably premature to formulate specific recommendations in the case of UNDP, but it at least needs to adapt its internal agenda of priorities (for example, the Evaluation Programme). Perhaps the effects of the political pressures inevitably felt by the staff of the regional bureaus could be mitigated by strengthening the TAD. In any event, a valuable first step could be explicit recognition by the UNDP's Governing Council that environmental degradation impedes progress toward meeting basic needs, and a clear acknowledgement by management and staff that environmental responsibility should fall not just to UNEP, but to the development planners themselves.

Notes

1. *UNDP 1976-1977 and Beyond,* pamphlet, 1977, page 8.

2. United Nations Document DP/261, "Role and Activities of UNDP," A note by the Administrator of UNDP to the Governing Council, Twenty-Fourth Session, June, 1977, p. 4.

3. Ibid., p. 20.

4. A draft was submitted to UNEP, in late 1977, of "Development of a Methodology Model for Integrated Analysis of Environmental Effects Related to the Development of a Hydrographic Basin," Organization of American States, Department of Regional Development, Washington, D.C. (1977).

5. Several other of the Special Projects of the OAS's Department of Scientific Affairs are noteworthy. One project in the Basic Sciences Unit is a special study on the development of arid and semiarid zones. The OAS is stimulating and coordinating applied research of institutions in Argentina, Chile, Peru, Haiti, and Mexico to retard the advance of the desert, to recover the degraded surfaces in order to attain optimal and sustained production, and to take overall advantage of the natural resources.

6. In fact, UNDP Resident Representatives, who also represent UNEP, do have a formal procedure to follow regarding all projects with environmental components, namely, to advise UNEP and keep it informed. This procedure includes sending to UNEP, as they become available, the draft Country Programme, the finalized Country Programme, and copies of Programme Management Plans. UNEP itself has four regional Resident Representatives in Beirut, Nairobi, Mexico City, and Bangkok. UNEP's Executive Director frankly acknowledges very limited capacity to respond to this vast flow of national country program documentation.

5

The European Development Fund

The European Development Fund (EDF) is dealt with separately because as a financing institution it is unlike any of the others examined here. The EDF is administered by one of the departments (Directorate General VIII) of the Commission of the European Community (with no separate legal personality but enjoying financial autonomy). It could be regarded as institutionally somewhere between the World Bank and the United Nations Development Programme (UNDP). In its variety of facilities and its flexibility it is not wholly dissimilar to the World Bank Group. Yet in its preponderant stress on grant aid (a large proportion of which are small-scale preinvestment projects) and its decentralized institutional structure, it parallels the UNDP.

The nine members of the European Economic Community (EEC) concluded in the 1975 Lome Convention an agreement with forty-six African, Caribbean, and Pacific (ACP) states that provides for duty free access to markets and financial and technical cooperation. (The number has since grown to fifty-two.) The Lome Convention—which followed the Yaounde Conventions between the six original European Economic Community members and eighteen, later nineteen, African states—contained some fundamental innovations, especially regarding the stabilization of export earnings, which reflect a new EEC policy towards producers of raw materials.

Under the heading of financial and technical cooperation, the EEC agreed in 1975 to provide 3,000 million European Units of Account (EUA) (about $3,750 million) over the five-year period of the present convention, to be made up of 2,100 million EUA for grants, 430 million EUA for loans on special terms, 95 million EUA for risk capital, and 374 million EUA for the stabilization of export earnings.[1] In addition, a further 390 million EUAs were to be made available for loans from the European Investment Bank, which acts principally as a development bank *within* the European Economic Community.

If the EDF is to be described as having an institutional personality between the World Bank and the UNDP, in terms of environmental awareness and procedures it is certainly much closer to the latter than the former. The EDF has apparently not altered its basis for judging projects since its detailed listing of eleven loan criteria appeared in 1973, without mentioning the environment.

There is no reference in EDF's constitution or terms of reference to the environment, nor is any environmental impact statement required in the project appraisal process. As with the regional development banks and the UNDP, a general consciousness of environmental issues was found among Fund officials interviewed, but also a reluctance to accept that specific procedures of environmental assessment, or additional staff with specific biological or ecological expertise, were appropriate in relation to EDF projects.

The parallel between the EDF and UNDP as regards decentralized structure and decision-making on loans and grants produces similar problems for any central assessment or standard setting function. There is an EDF office now in forty-two of the ACP parties to the new Lome convention. These offices are staffed with economists, agronomists, engineers, and so forth, who participate with national officials in the preparation of loan and grant proposals. At the beginning of each five-year convention period, a programming mission headed by the director general for development cooperation visits each ACP country and negotiates, in outline, a five-year program of grants and loans. In the course of the convention period, the committee of the EDF meets about two or three times a month to evaluate upcoming projects prepared on the basis of the outline program.

Apparently it is possible to raise environmental questions at this latter stage, but it seemed clear from interviews at the fund that this would be too late in the project preparation process to produce any fundamental redesign of a faulty project.

Because projects are jointly prepared by EDF field staff and national officials, negotiation of agreement on the project shape and technical approach adopted occurs simultaneously with project appraisal. It would therefore seem essential for the EDF to develop a capacity for environmental assessment at the country level in the project preparation phase.

The EDF appears to have a rather low level of environmental awareness and was a difficult agency to assess. Officers of the fund insisted that because grants and loans were negotiated jointly with the ACP partners, project documents could not be released for examination without permission of the national governments.

On the other hand, the European Commission's Consumer Affairs and Environment Protection Service referred, in its second *Action Programme on the Environment*, to the possibility of drawing ACP states' attention to environmental matters, and devoting special attention to projects aimed at increasing the value of renewable local resources and developing the technologies most suited to the specific requirements of the ACP countries.[2] The service is currently engaged in discussions with the EDF as to how these considerations may be incorporated into the second Lome Convention, and into terms of reference of the programming missions as they prepare the outline program of loans and grants for the period 1980-1985.

It is clearly vital that environmental guidelines and where possible agreements regarding assessment procedures be prepared at the earliest possible stage in these negotiations. Here it seems most desirable that the EDF work closely with the Brussels office of the ACP states, as well as with individual countries through the fund's field offices and through preparatory missions.

Notes

1. With the new accessions to the Convention, the EDF total has been increased to 3,057.5 million EUA.

2. See *Second Action Programme on the Environment*, European Communities R/70 e/77 (Env 36), Annex pp. 259-63.

Part II
Some Sectoral Policies and Activities of the Nine Agencies

Introduction

The previous chapters have dealt with general environmental procedures and practices in the nine institutions under review. Identified strengths and weaknesses are now examined in four substantive areas of activity.

The four sectors: human settlements, energy, water resources, and forestry, were chosen for a variety of reasons. First, they are diverse yet closely interconnected. They also represent sectors that include areas of traditional lending as well as those focusing on meeting the recent interest in basic human needs. Third, while development in several of the sectors, for example, water and dams, commercial forestry, and some energy projects, often damage the physical environment, work in each sector, such as lending for fuelwood projects, community water supply, and shelter improvement are development schemes designed to directly improve the physical and human environment. Certainly these criteria also cover other sectors that might have been picked. Most of the institutions under review lend, indeed lend principally, for industrial or other infrastructure projects that potentially pollute or otherwise damage the environment. These sectors were avoided, however, primarily because the strategies necessary for introducing environmental controls are known, and can be practiced if the will exists to apply them. This does not, however, minimize either the importance of these sectors or the difficulty of securing acceptance of effective controls.

Before examining each of our four sectors, several additional introductory comments are in order.

First, the fields of activity chosen do not necessarily divide into well-defined project areas as practiced by the lending institutions under review. There is a great deal of overlap, and in a number of cases the choice of where to discuss things may appear arbitrary. For example, discussion of the effects of hydropower fits into either water resources or energy (the former was chosen); colonization projects into forestry or human settlements (the latter); urban water supply into settlements or water resources (the latter); and there are others as well. The aim was to choose a nexus of major environmental concern within the categories and use this as the guide.

Second, the sectors differ considerably in the importance of the roles of the lending institutions. Community water supply development is approximately 90 percent funded from within countries while only 10 percent comes from external sources. Even in this case, however, banks can effect a leverage role by picking the projects that appeal the most to them and that have the best chance of success. In any event, it is not to be assumed that changes in the ways in which multilateral agencies act will automatically effect changes in the way countries view sustainable development. The role of the banks in any sector will be that of a supporting, though important, actor.

   Third, the sectors differ in their susceptibility to normal or traditional economic or financial rate-of-return calculations. With many institutions having both regular and soft loan facilities, it is clear that tests other than a strict economic rate of return are applied. It is through the use of these latter criteria that loans or grants most directly concerned with meeting basic human needs are justified. It is hoped that the concept of sustainability in development will be recognized by readers of this report as a thread that runs through each sectoral chapter and, indeed, binds them together as a whole.

6 Human Settlements: Urban Shelter and Rural Colonization

It is clear that analysis of the environmental impact of the multilateral banks' and technical assistance agencies' work in the area of human settlements presents problems distinctly different from those encountered in the other areas of sectoral study. In the first instance, this is because more than in any of the other areas reviewed, so many loans and project components (such as those labeled "public utilities") are really inseparable from settlements of one kind or another. Human settlements lending in its broadest sense may include the financing of roads, electricity supply and transmission, telecommunications, port and harbor facilities, industry, agriculture, and education. In short, the case can be made that all development activity directly or indirectly affects settlement patterns, the human condition, and the human environment.

It would be difficult in the extreme to assess the effects of even a few of all these types of projects on human settlements. Tracing through the effects of upgrading a road between two existing towns would be a massive task in itself, involving not only questions of resource use in the construction of the road, but questions of siting, of spreading infectious diseases or parasites, of construction standards, of technologies, of relocation of people in the near- or long-term, and myriad other effects. Likewise, a description of all the major and minor impacts of education, employment, electrification, or other projects which, to a greater or lesser degree, affect land use and settlement patterns, was not possible. Quantifying and judging the value of this activity, or evaluating the extent to which banks and technical assistance agencies have succeeded in grappling with these issues was also impossible.

The Urban Shelter Crisis

The mushrooming growth of cities in the developing world has produced an appalling deterioration in human environments. According to 1975 World Bank estimates, 190 million urban poor lacked access to the basic amenities of potable water, sanitation, medical services, and housing, and their numbers are increasing at an estimated rate of 11 million persons a year.[1] Under these circumstances, periodic epidemics of cholera take 200 to 300 lives per week. Tuberculosis affects about 10 percent of the population, and 50 percent of the children of these slums are affected by malnutrition.[2] Cities are so choked and urban services so overloaded (Calcutta's waste disposal system, for example, serves ten times the population for which it was designed) that the cities cease to function at all, and it becomes meaningless to distinguish between the quality of the environment and the quality of life.

The countries whose settlements have the worst environments are generally those with the fastest growing cities. Ironically, they are often the countries where the rural population is still predominant (between 60 and 80 percent) and where the annual rate of rural population growth is above 1 percent. If China is excluded, this group of countries contains over half (54 percent) of the population of the Third World. The group includes India (where 75 percent of the population is still rural), Nigeria, several Arab countries (particularly the UAR), and countries like Viet Nam, Turkey, and the Philippines. Most of the small Latin American states also fall into this category. Urban population in these countries tends to grow at over 4 percent a year, in many at over 5 percent. This produces an almost unthinkable doubling in city size every fourteen to eighteen years. Clearly the implications of such torrential urban growth for the provision of the most basic environmental amenities of shelter and services are staggering. The problems are already overwhelming responsible authorities; they will soon be totally unmanageable if present policies persist.

Perhaps because of their very scale, and because they are often the by-product of other higher priorities of policy, like increasing agricultural productivity or improving surface communications between centers, urban settlement problems as such have seldom attracted the attention of policy makers. Whether intentionally or from lack of any overall perception, governments and international agencies tend to look at these problems as sectoral issues, as do business communities and organized labor. Despite the many recommendations for national action approved by governments at the U.N. Human Settlements Conference (Habitat) Conference in Vancouver in 1976, very few governments have taken steps to implement even a few of them.

It is unclear why urban problems have been so generally ignored until recently in national and international discussions. Certainly, (despite substantial investments in communications, power, roads, and other aspects of urban infrastructure) national and international agencies pursue other priorities for investment than the provision of better and more sanitary living conditions. Two years after the U.N. Conference on Human Settlements, discussions still lack the specificity that the problems require. As a recent International Institute for Environment and Development (IIED) assessment of nineteen countries in Asia, Africa, Latin America, and the Middle East reveals, practically no country has adequately defined its human settlements policy and very few countries have attempted to implement them. This despite clear indications that the number of people living in pathetic and degrading slum and squatter settlements is going to increase, as several countries move towards agglomerations of fifteen, twenty, and thirty million people: megalopoli that must pose—to put it in the most cynical of political terms—unforeseeable problems of public order around the centers of national government.

To provide conditions of even the most minimal environmental acceptability (employment, shelter, water and sewer services, for example) to those who live in miserable and sanitarily dangerous dwellings would require an investment beyond the capacity of most economies to sustain. However, the apparent scale of the problem varies greatly with the approach adopted. There exist technologies and resources in every region of the world that could be developed with rapidity, and in many cases with great economic benefit to the region. Suitable raw materials can be used to develop simple building industries with a very positive impact on employment. Urban conditions in the Third World cry out for experimental approaches, for targets and standards that are flexible enough to vary widely with circumstances. By now, planners, policy makers, the business community, and organized labor should realize that the developing city can never achieve tolerable environmental conditions if they insist on rigid standards, designed for wealthier societies, which include housing codes and regulations utterly remote from the economic and social realities faced by those who suffer the most degraded of community environments.

The Role of International Agencies

Because of the complexities involved in urban planning (a shanty town of five thousand people can spring up literally overnight) the amount of high-quality technical assistance the institutions could conceivably provide is dwarfed by the magnitude of the problems. In essence, the banks have had to deal largely with a given urban or rural settlement situation that can be affected only marginally by what these institutions attempt to do.

The IIED approach taken to settlements questions was therefore highly selective. Broad human settlements lending and policies of the institutions are considered and then three categories of projects that have the most direct impact on the most degraded or fragile environments which are—inevitably—those of the very poor are examined. First to be discussed are urban shelter projects; second, the banks' efforts to support a new settlement within an existing urban agglomeration with a site and service project (in this latter context shantytown upgrading is included); last to be discussed are rural settlements (a limited number of rural colonization projects are examined, recognizing, however, that such projects alone cannot measurably affect migration, even as they create new settlements).

In this review, the effort is made to establish whether living standards have been improved and whether these standards can be maintained or raised in the future. The attempt is also made to see if the projects are replicable on a wide scale; whether after initial aid from development agencies, countries will have the expertise and resources to pursue additional similar projects in significant numbers. Finally, the question of whether these projects can be upgraded in the future as incomes rise is examined.

One final point must be made before entering into the substance of these three areas of technical assistance and development lending. Primary responsibility for creating, upgrading, or otherwise determining the course of settlement patterns does not lie with the agencies studied. It rests with national and local governments and the people who will live in these towns, villages, and cities. If fault is found with the agencies either for not doing enough or for not achieving the results hoped for, the main criticism is implicitly of the governments, especially of larger countries, for not putting enough emphasis on human settlements issues, thereby allowing the settlements situation to have become so desperate and degraded. Development banks can only operate in a supporting capacity. Even if they were to devote all of their time, effort, and money to the three sectors of housing, sites and services, and rural colonization, let alone to basically essential public infrastructure, these resources would still be inadequate to allow them to alter conditions dramatically.

Urbanization Policy and Projects at the International Lending Agencies

Policy and Projects at the World Bank

The 1971-1976 period produced a very marked increase in the total amount of approved loans by the World Bank Group (an annual average of US $4,643.1 million) and major changes in the sectoral breakdown of lending. A relative decrease in lending in what were considered by the Bank Group the "economic sectors" left, in theory at least, more funds for the so-called "social sectors" among which human settlement components can be found. The shift to the categories of settlements projects selected for this study was, however, not of impressive magnitude. Lending for urbanization projects, mainly for sites and services, amounted to $314 million or 1.4 percent of total lending for the 1971-1976 period. It represented an average of $62.8 million per year, reaching a peak of $113 million in 1973-1974 and declining to $79.6 million in 1975-1976. However as indicated in table 6-1, the picture at the World Bank is changing rapidly. Account must be taken not only of the substantially increased commitments in 1977 and 1978 but also the substantial start-up time required to develop capacity in the Bank and to convince governments to develop such loan requests. According to Bank officials they now have eighty urbanization projects in the lending program for the next five years.

It is a safe estimate that close to 200 million people today live in desperate urban slum conditions.[3] The World Bank's actual annual allocation of $62.8 million for urban projects, even if presumptively matched by a local contribution of $10.00 per person, can provide only $3.14 per person per year to improve the shelters of these urban slum dwellers. Yet in the opinion of a

Table 6-1
Project Financing for Urban Shelter, 1971-1976

Agency[a]	Number of Projects[b]	Amount ($ millions)	% of Total Lending
IBRD[c]	16	273.9	1.1%
IDB	6	111.45	1.8%
AsDB[d]	1	1.15	.04%
CDB	35	13.4	12.1%
EDF	—	15.0	1.6%
UNDP	—	27.0	1.6%

[a]ADB, BADEA, and OAS acknowledged no lending or technical assistance specifically to this sector.

[b]Includes only projects directly related to urban housing (does not include water supply and waste disposal).

[c]In 1977, however, the IBRD committed an additional $311.7 million and in 1978, $465.1 million.

[d]The AsDB made a $20.5 million loan for low-income housing in April 1977.

number of experts who have worked to design minimal shelter, it costs $1000 to $1500 per unit to prepare a site, service it with rudimentary water supply and waste disposal and other essential services, and purchase materials for small, basic, self-constructed shelter. This gives some indication of the enormity of the housing problem; bleaker still comes the realization that, even if *all* of the World Bank's financing were allocated to basic housing amenity, excluding actual construction, these poorest elements of global society would have at their disposal about $232 per person per year to upgrade their shelters. It is quite clear, then, that external assistance alone will not solve the problem. It should therefore be applied in ways most likely to stimulate government and local action. The World Bank intends by 1982 to allocate as much as 10 percent of its resources to urban projects.

Housing. The World Bank has rejected housing projects, as such, as have all other multilateral lending institutions studied, with the exceptions of the Asian Development Bank (AsDB), which has financed two projects in this area, and the Caribbean Development Bank (CDB), which has funded a number of very small housing projects. Housing projects are not considered by the Bank because these projects serve the urban middle class which has alternative sources of credit. However, by providing a *lower* level of service, the IBRD (or World Bank) has also spread its limited resources further than if housing were constructed. The IBRD has recognized the fundamental truth that the vast majority of people have always constructed their own homes, for want of any other alternative, to their own standards and that collective government efforts have been most useful for providing reasonably priced services, not housing itself.

Site and Service and Slum Upgrading Programs. The World Bank initiated its site and service projects with a project in Senegal in fiscal year 1973. In 1975, after funding several more such projects, the Bank produced a Sector Policy Paper on the subject. This was very general but nonetheless set the parameters for future refinement of the concept. This approach is being adopted by the other banks.

The World Bank has found that its sites and services projects generally cannot directly benefit the poorest fifth of the urban population.[4] These people generally have no permanent jobs and therefore no savings and little income and cannot pay for even these minimal services. Upgrading schemes can reach as low as the tenth percentile of urban income distribution, but seldom lower. Above these very low income levels, however, urban people *can* afford to pay for minimum infrastructure and *can* provide their own house more cheaply than would be the case if it were provided by any development project. This group is identified as people in roughly the twentieth to sixtieth percentiles of urban income distribution who are able to afford one of usually two preferred levels of service. A third level of site and service, with substantially better amenities, may be made available to higher income groups. This is often arranged so that they in effect subsidize poorer urbanites, while helping to avoid creating ghettoes of low-income residents.

The principle involved here is to recover full costs so that funds may be available to future site and service projects. In practice, nearly the full cost of the project must be borne by the participants, which implies that service components be minimal: at a level that people can afford and desire, yet upgradable as incomes rise. Construction and design standards must be flexible, depending on such variables as absolute income levels, local culture, and environmental conditions (climate, terrain, susceptibility to storms and earthquakes, and so forth).

The World Bank's Sector Policy Paper did not explicitly mention the location of site and service projects, but the Bank quickly realized that a location as close as possible to sources of income and transportation was necessary if the participants were to be near their jobs. In effect, the site and service approach could help to minimize sprawl.

In general, the World Bank has attempted to correct some of the earlier mistakes in its site and service projects. For example, as indicated above, some initial projects did not adequately consider employment conditions, and in seeking to keep project costs low sometimes located participants on the perimeter of the city. Participants became isolated from city life and had to spend too much time and money getting into town to work or market. Future projects have been located within a few kilometers of the urban center. Many recent projects, such as that in Malaysia in 1976, have sites for light industry and commerce to increase employment opportunities.

In El Salvador, a study revealed that the incidence of respiratory diseases climbed relative to general population growth during the housing construction phase of the sites and services project. The World Bank now makes it a policy to provide low interest construction loans so that participants can build their shelter faster. The same study revealed that the incidence of infectious water-borne diseases did not decline as rapidly as expected after hygienic water and waste disposal facilities were installed. This problem was traced to a lack of nutritional and sanitary education. This basic knowledge is now generally provided to women in World Bank projects. The low interest loans and practical information for women are clearly distinct environmental improvements. The El Salvador study points out the need for official post-audits which have not yet been carried out.

The World Bank has also recognized that in many instances it is cheaper and preferable to bring services to existing slums rather than to provide new sites. In this whole area, the World Bank has benefited from the previous experience of other international bodies, for example, the World Council of Churches and national and local authorities. Upgrading existing slums avoids delays over the location of sites and services projects and delicate negotiations concerning proper construction standards. It also becomes unnecessary to purchase new urban land. A number of recent projects, such as those in Ivory Coast, India, and the Philippines, have emphasized upgrading rather than creating new settlements, and the Bank will continue this trend in the future. Since 1972, the World Bank has invested in twenty-one site and service or urban upgrading projects, for a total commitment of about $470 million. Over 90,000 families are living in World Bank site and service project areas; many more are living in low-income settlements benefited by World Bank upgrading projects.

Governments have, however, often resisted upgrading. The general response has been to bulldoze these informal settlements away. The World Bank approach has been to recognize the investment made in shelter in these settlements and work to increase rather than to raze it. Bank staff said that involvement in these projects was limited initially not so much by lack of money as by borrower failure to appreciate the need for and practicality of this solution and lack of implementation capacity as well.

But site and service and urban slum upgrading projects are far from ideal solutions to the problem of degraded urban environments. So far, the poorest fifth of the urban population has not been reached and no one in any of the banks studied knows any way to reach them, short of abandoning cost recovery and with it, project replicability in the long run. In the back of Bank officials' minds is, of course, the bottomless pit aspect of directly subsidizing housing. Governments themselves simply cannot provide free housing, and certainly multilateral development financing agencies should not be expected to do so. Furthermore, funds have not been allocated nor has enough pressure been put on governments to address such touchy political issues as land reform or the recapture of value added by urban land scarcity and speculation, which more insidiously threaten replicability. Failure to make significant progress on these difficult political issues makes land costs soar in urban areas. As a precondition for dealing with the most acute aspects of their urban shelter crisis, governments must exert public control over land development, create land banks, bring urban land into public ownership, or employ progressive land tax and land use policies. However, in fairness it must be noted that even governments which have progressed with such measures (such as Tanzania and Zambia) are still faced with intractible urban problems.

World Bank officials told the IIED project team that at best, the revolving funds created by its International Development Association (IDA) loans with full cost recovery will be sufficient to shelter adequately one-third of the estimated future migrants, an ambitious target, to be sure. Other funds will be necessary to improve the existing housing stock and meet the needs of the majority of urban migrants. If human and environmental degradation is really to be lessened, problems such as land reform, recapture of value added, creation of jobs, appropriate technology, better redistribution of the fruits of growth, and sheer spending levels *must* be more effectively considered.[5]

Colonization. The World Bank has recently (January 1978) made available a policy paper on colonization.[6] This paper analyzes Bank projects between 1962 and 1974. Surprisingly, the major cause of failure—moving into new ecological regimes where soils, rainfall, pests, and diseases make productive work extraordinarily difficult—was not mentioned. Instead, the paper says that benefits have tended to be exaggerated and costs have escalated, a less insightful way of saying that environmental conditions differed so much from case to case that estimates based on past experience were generally inapplicable. Nevertheless, the World Bank will continue to invest in colonization projects.

Much of the history of man is written in spontaneous colonization of new agricultural frontiers. Today, the frontiers are limited to rapidly falling tropical forests. Settlers move to accessible forest fringes where they cut and burn trees on a small plot (slash and burn or swidden agriculture), destroying high-value wood in the process. After a few cropping seasons, characteristically weak tropical forest soils are exhausted, their few nutrients absorbed by plants or leached below annual crop root levels by heavy seasonal rain. Soil structure deteriorates in the intense light and heat. Pests and diseases, held in check by the vast former diversity of plant life and the presence of predators, multiply with the disappearance of the forest and concentration on a few species of agriculturally useful plants. The land must therefore be abandoned after a few croppings and the farmers move to cut a new area. The World Bank estimates that approximately 200 million settlers cultivate 300 million hectares using this system of agriculture.

According to World Bank estimates in the colonization policy paper, 75 percent of colonization in the tropics is spontaneous. Government assisted or directed colonization, with or without outside capital, constitutes the remaining

25 percent of colonization projects. Governments are increasingly wary of planned settlement schemes because of past failures, but faced with the politically painful alternative of redistributing agricultural land, they still invest in colonization.

Like governments, the development banks become involved because they believe they have little choice. Colonization schemes are the kind of high-cost, urgent development projects for which bank assistance is often most sought by member governments. Direct participation, even despite the risks involved, does give the banks more leverage to insist on as much environmental soundness as possible. Finally, for the World Bank at least, colonization projects, despite their high cost, involve attempts to help the poorest farmers and landless peasants, and therefore receive close attention.

The classic problem of planned settlement projects is the unplanned cutting of timber or scrub on land that cannot sustain agriculture or cattle. This is done by "unofficial" settlers, whether in areas around colonization projects (as in Brazil, Colombia, and Nepal), or along access routes leading to colonies (particularly in Brazil, Colombia, and Bolivia). This problem can be minimized if access roads are not built until a settlement is well established. However, this solution contradicts the basic theory that (in the main) the absence of roads retarded agricultural development on the frontier.

Another problem of planned colonization is avoiding clearing forests along streams and on steep slopes, thus avoiding destructive erosion. In the World Bank-financed Caqueta settlement project, a zone set aside as a forest reserve was badly pillaged by settlers, and riverside trees in the project area were cut down. There just was no force available capable of controlling illegal settler cutting. To one degree or another, this seems to have been the fate of surrounding forests in every colonization project.

Aside from the damage that settlers can inflict on the environment, the environment works against the settlers. Cropping systems adapted to different soil, pest, and climate regimes fail in the new settlements. Cattle fall prey to new pests, and people are subjected to new diseases. It is not surprising, given the difficulties that this new environment presents to colonizers, that anticipated benefits of colonization projects have been overestimated.

Between 1962 and 1971, the World Bank committed about $360 million in twenty-five colonization projects, or about 5 percent of all agricultural lending. Since 1973, nine more projects have been financed with a commitment of almost $100 million. Much of the money has been invested in Indonesia and Malaysia, but several loans have been in Africa (Ethiopia, Rwanda, Senegal, and Cameroon, to name a few) and in Latin America (Colombia, Trinidad and Tobago).

The most environmentally sophisticated colonization project funded by the World Bank is the 1977 Indonesia transmigration project. The project is designed to protect slopes from erosion by not clearing certain areas and by planting cleared slopes with rubber and legumes. Participants are to be trained in soil conservation techniques. Flatland is to be cleared by hand and planted with crops that soil surveys indicate may not be sustainable in the long run, but that will provide incomes until the rubber trees mature and the rubber plantation expands. Cattle will be raised on legume fodder planted on fallow fields. Although none of the cropping systems have been tested in the field, the population of the inner islands of Indonesia is recognized by the Bank to be reaching or surpassing levels of ecological sustainability and a risky expansion into marginal agricultural lands is thus unavoidable. Second, agronomists at the Bank believe that at least one of the cropping designs will work, providing the participants with an income.

The settlement itself was designed in linear fashion to compromise on costs of infrastructure and distance to fields. This plan was designed around the wants of the settlers and with their active participation, and it allows for future improvement or upgrading. Clinics and schools are to be provided, and roof-top rain collectors may eventually be replaced with piped water supply. Measures are being taken against malaria in the area as an integral part of the project.

This World Bank colonization project should give people a better standard of living than if they remained landless in Java or Sumatra. Moreover, it uses agricultural techniques that should prove sustainable.

Policy and Lending at the Inter-American Development Bank

Housing, Urban Improvement, and Colonization. Between 1961 and 1966, the Inter-American Development Bank (IDB) devoted almost one-fifth of its resources to housing and urban development projects. However this activity fell to 3 percent of total project lending in the 1967 to 1971 period and to 2.4 percent between 1972 and 1976. In fact, new IDB lending for housing was discontinued after 1968. There were two major reasons for the dramatic decline in IDB lending in this sector. The Bank found that loans were directed toward middle-class urban groups, who had alternative sources of financing. Such lending, the IDB felt, was justified neither on economic nor social grounds.

That at least is the official picture. However, the cut-off of funds for housing coincided with the closing of the Social Progress Trust Fund (SPTF), of which IDB was the administrator. The SPTF was a creature of the Kennedy administration, and consisted of funds authorized by the U.S. Congress for Latin American aid. These funds could only be used for social development projects such as community water supply and sanitation and housing for low-income groups through assistance to self-help housing. During the years in which the so-called low-income housing projects were financed by the IDB, there was practically no commitment to rural housing, and housing standards were sufficiently high in the urban areas to make them unreachable for the vast majority of the population.

At the end of 1967, the IDB had no clear position on human settlements or housing. In a document circulated at the end of 1975 ("Urban Development: Basic Operational Guidelines"), the IDB recognized "that its financial capacity is far exceeded by the financial requirements of its member countries to carry out their programs for urban development." Following this pronouncement, the IDB attached high priority first, to providing technical assistance for the formulation of national and regional urban policies of institutional betterment, to training of professional and technical personnel, to research studies and to project preparation; and second, to finance specific investment projects in water, sewage disposal and drainage, infrastructure services such as electric power, communications, urbanization works and transportation, and industrial and economic projects of high productivity in urban areas.

In 1973 and 1977, the IDB developed three integrated urban development projects (which, however, fall outside the scope of this review). It should be noted, parenthetically perhaps, that while experience with those integrated projects was on the whole encouraging, this approach involves so much administrative time and complexity for the amount of money involved that it may be abandoned.[7]

As previously noted, very little colonization work has yet been done by the regional development banks. The one with the longest experience is the IDB, with twenty projects financed, most of them (thirteen, worth $84 million) in its first five years of operation. The IDB financed one project per year in 1970, 1971, 1973, and 1976 for a commitment of $50.6 million. Total commitment, 1961-1976, is $163.5 million.

A recent IDB colonization project seemed to have all the necessary environmental safeguards. The existing tree cover was surveyed and found to be unsuitable for commercial exploitation, although some of the wood could be used for building houses and fences. Steep slopes and creek beds were left forested for erosion and run-off control. A soil survey was undertaken to see if it was suitable for cattle production and the type of agriculture envisaged. The settlers at the site were relocated into towns so that water and electricity could be better provided. However, no studies of insects or pests in the region were carried out, the prevalence of endemic diseases or their vectors was not determined, and no sociological studies (or even conversations with project participants) were conducted concerning relocating the settlers into nuclear villages.

The soil survey said that the soil was "intensely weathered," "severely leached," "lateritic," and of generally poor quality. Considering the rainfall of the area (2500 mm/yr), there is reason to believe the soil will become compacted and unmanageable, especially if overcropped or overgrazed. Nowhere was it evident that the results of the soil survey were taken into account in determining the type of agriculture and the yield that could be sustained at the site. Early yields of beans, rice, and corn did not reach anticipated levels, and the IDB has now advocated planting tree crops. In fact, the cattle population at its peak will reach one to the acre, a figure that might well be too high. The project documents, furthermore, do not indicate how the population will be limited to that figure.

The severely geometrical layout of the villages was not only decided upon without consulting the future inhabitants, but the farmers have now found that the villages are too far from their fields. The families consequently live in the villages, enjoying the benefits of potable water and electricity, while the farmers live in hovels closer to their farms.

Human Settlements Investment at the
Asian Development Bank

Between January 1968, when the Asian Development Bank (AsDB) signed its first loan, and November 1977, only 2 out of a total of 291 loans made to twenty-three countries by the AsDB were described as for urban development. This represents 0.55 percent of the total lending activities of the AsDB to this time.

The AsDB is the only regional bank besides the Caribbean Development Bank (CDB) which now makes housing loans. It approved a loan of $20.5 million for the Sha Tin housing project to help finance a portion of the foreign currency costs (including building materials like cement and equipment) of about eight thousand apartments and community service buildings in a new town development in Hong Kong. The AsDB mission sent to assess the project noted "the effort to improve the environment by improvements introduced in the layout of the housing blocks, in the estate layout and landscaping, and through pollution control measures." However, Hong Kong's minimum norms for floor space are so mean, at 35 square feet per capita excluding kitchen, balconies, and bathrooms (19'10" X 15' net floor space for a nine person apartment), that when incorporated in buildings of up to twenty-eight stories they represent a questionable improvement on the environment of the low-income families previously living in squatter settlements or on boats.

Aside from one additional loan of $1.15 million for urban planning and a number of loans for urban water supply and waste disposal (reviewed in chapter 7), the AsDB has made no other loans of direct impact on urban settlements. The AsDB has attempted no sites and services projects, integrated urban development projects, or slum upgrading projects.

The AsDB has, however, supported a number of integrated rural development projects and several colonization projects. From a review of a selection of appraisal reports, the AsDB can be characterized as fairly sensitive to the needs of project participants. In several instances, socioeconomic surveys were undertaken before the projects were begun, and in at least one instance, participants helped design the layout of the new settlement. The settlers wanted traditional housing with space for gardens as well as the basic amenities of water supply and roads. Although this dispersed settlement pattern increased the cost of the project, both the government and the AsDB agreed to it.

Human Settlements Policy and Lending at the
Caribbean Development Bank

The Caribbean Development Bank (CDB) has invested a sizeable proportion of its funds in the housing sector. Between 1970 and 1976, 12 percent of the $111.3 million worth of approved loans were for low-income housing. The average rate of lending is about $2 million per year, but this figure is somewhat misleading because commitments have been growing rapidly since 1974-1975.

New loans totaling $2.9 million were approved in 1976, providing for construction of 728 houses at a unit cost of almost $4,000. In 1976, three housing projects were cancelled by borrower governments, perhaps because this "urban working class housing" is too expensive. As with the IDB, the reason that a housing, rather than a site and service, approach is taken may be related to the fact that the U.S. Agency for International Development (USAID) has provided capital and was consulted in revising the CDB's Housing Program.

Human Settlements Policy and Lending at the
African Development Bank and the Arab Bank for
Economic Development of Africa

In the case of both the African Development Bank (ADB) and the Arab Bank for Economic Development of Africa (BADEA), there has been no specific investment in human settlements projects which would raise the environmental impact of urban or rural settlements policy. However, loans for water and urban infrastructure absorb significant shares of the funds committed.

Human Settlements Policy and Lending at
the European Development Fund

Of some $2,500 million of loans and grants approved by the European Development Fund (EDF) in eighteen countries between 1960 and 1975, no loans for housing are evident and the Fund had no housing policy. Because the EDF's policy is to respond to requests from governments and because few of the forty-six governments that signed the Lomé Convention appeared interested in giving priority to human settlements, aid in this sector has seldom been requested. At the end of 1977, only three projects related to human settlements as defined in this chapter had been approved: the Dwangera improvement scheme in the Nairobi metropolitan area; a squatter settlement upgrading project in Kingston, Jamaica; and a housing scheme with very low standards, divided among different cities of Ethiopia. The total financial commitment of the EDF for the three projects was equivalent to $8.5 million, or about 0.85 percent of the financial loan and grant commitments of the Fund in one year. Since 1977, however, a considerably greater commitment to housing projects has been in evidence.

At present, the EDF has very few staff members involved in the human settlements sector, although a housing policy paper for the European Economic Commission is being planned. The feeling prevails among EDF staff that policy will largely be influenced by World Bank policies, and that unless the second Lomé agreement strongly supports human settlements programs, the situation will remain unchanged.

Human Settlements Policy and Lending at
the United Nations Development Programme

Technical assistance provided by the United Nations Development Programme (UNDP) to twenty-two countries was examined for this study.[8] Most country programs cover the period 1972-1977, although for some countries the period 1972-1978 or 1977-1981 is covered. In all cases, the country programs follow the objectives and priorities of each country's national development plan. Of course, the aid requested by each government to the UNDP does not reflect, in percentage terms, the total national involvement in particular economic or social sectors.

Specific aid for housing and urban development was requested by only two countries. It amounted to 0.16 percent of all aid given by UNDP to those twenty-two countries between 1961 and 1976 according to country programs. However, in the aid requested of UNDP for other sectors and programs, the human settlements situation and the general condition of the human habitat are mentioned. Aid for cooperative housing planning and the physical planning of housing was included under "infrastructure" by Tanzania.

It is difficult to assess the real extent of settlements-related aid because of the wide variety of categories. Nevertheless, it seems clear that total aid for housing, habitat, and environmentally oriented human settlements programs and projects represent a derisory volume of resources.

Summary of Findings and Recommendations

As a result of visits to the World Bank, IDB, CDB, UNDP, EDF, and the U.N. Centre for Housing, Building and Planning, certain conclusions emerge quite clearly from discussions with officials and technicians in those organizations.

1. Resources devoted to human settlements programs are pitifully short. No government in the developing world is making all the necessary investments nor are most adopting even the most rudimentary settlements policies and standards. Despite the Habitat Conference and the catastrophic state of human settlements around the world, international agencies and bilateral programs have other priorities. Even when, in sectoral projects, attention could be paid to human settlements policies and standards, the indifference of governments and most international development agencies is clear.

2. Coordination among most financing institutions is almost nonexistent. There are general meetings for the purpose of coordination on a *country-by-country basis,* but in general, project officials and directors of specialized sections know little of what is being done by other organizations, much less of what these other agencies are planning to do in the next few years.[9] In present circumstances, agencies will continue to formulate contradictory policy recommendations. Quite often a lending agency reorients the objectives and priorities of the technical assistance agency which has been working on a particular project for one, two, or more years. *Coordination at the level of policy recommendations is urgent*, and the urgency of achieving optimal results on investment is increased, given the very limited resources available. There are numerous instances where one international agency has helped a government to prepare an urban master plan which a lending development bank has disregarded. It should be possible to agree on a frame of reference that integrates the main directives (or lines) of investment. *A minimum of order at the territorial level is essential.* This calls, of course, for an exercise in integrated programming.

3. Aid in settlements-related projects is being transferred to countries where national institutions have had little or no experience in the field, and thus lack indispensable knowledge and contacts (in their own coutry or elsewhere) to ask for the appropriate help. This creates the danger that untested and improvised settlements projects of international agencies become the background for national human settlement policies simply because most governments have not given attention to the problem or because they think it is so unmanageable that they adopt a laissez-faire attitude. Project conception and execution are generally paternalistic and show little concern for basic participation despite the fact that participation is frequently discussed. This is especially disastrous in the case of most colonization settlements that occur spontaneously with environmentally devastating results and only the shortest of short-term benefits.

4. *The international agencies should recognize the importance of the leadership position which they are best equipped* to assume. Although loans and grants of the international agencies to the less developed countries for the construction of human settlements amount to a very small percentage of the basic investments required, they constitute, in the very poor countries, a high percentage of the total investment in the sector. As a general rule, therefore, the poorer the country the greater can be the impact of international agencies. Standards for the construction of urban settlements, plans, and priorities will continue to receive little serious attention unless a leading role is played by the agencies.

5. The political explanation for this disastrous state of affairs seems to be that there is no organized constituency to speak on behalf of human settlements programs. Governments still regard problems of housing and shelter as purely local, to be handled at the lowest level of responsibility. In almost all of the international agencies studied, with the exception of the World Bank (where, according to Bank staff, one-fourth of all new staff positions are in the Urban Projects Division, and where lending levels are programmed to increase dramatically in the next five years), "settlements" has not clearly emerged as a sectoral area to which a segment of staff and management commit time and energy. Finally, of course, the victims of this chaotic situation are the millions who have neither the training, resources, nor ability to advocate possible solutions effectively.

Notes

1. World Bank *Annual Report*, 1976, p. 19.
2. *The Urban Edge*, vol. 2, no. 1, January, 1978.
3. World Bank *Annual Report*, 1976, p. 19.
4. In a project in Guatemala cosponsored by the National Housing Bank of Guatemala and the World Bank, 35.5 percent of the low-income population could not afford the scheme. (See Marroquin, Hermes, ed., *El Problema de la Vivienda Popular in el Area Metropoliana de Guatemala*, 1978, pp. 262-263 and table I-z, p. 4.
5. As recently as 1976, governments identified these as the key problems confronting urban areas. See United Nations, *Report of Habitat: United Nations Conference on Human Settlements* (A/CONF. 70/15), New York, 1976, pp. 10-80, esp.
6. "Agricultural Land Settlement," A World Bank Issues Paper, January 1978.
7. The IDB is currently debating whether to fund similar projects in the future. The concept of integrated urban development should not be abandoned even though the burdens this type of project imposes are enormous. The IDB

could perhaps attempt to arrange cofinancing with other international agencies. Such a technique would impose greater hardship at first, for negotiations would have to be conducted with borrowers and cofinancers, but as cofinancers become aware of IDB objectives, they could carry out much of the negotiation and execution with IDB supervision. At the very least, the IDB should by prepared to refer borrowers interested in integrated urban development approaches to a variety of agencies that could coordinate their efforts to meet the goals.

8. Eighteen of these countries are included in a program of regional assessments of their national human settlements policies that is being undertaken in a separate project by IIED.

9. Agencies involved in financial aid for urban settlements seem to follow the leadership of the World Bank, but World Bank policies tend to focus on the effects, not the causes, of the situation, and do not appear to have been evaluated as a whole.

7

Energy Policies and Projects of the Multilateral Development Financing Institutions

The Need for a Radical Reappraisal

The central problem with development banks' energy aid is that, more than in any other sector studied, it has scarcely touched the world's poorest people. It has thus left them to use energy in ways highly destructive to their environment. As the number of rural poor grows and the price of fuel oil, especially kerosene, lifts out of their reach, these people rely increasingly upon the traditional energy sources of firewood or animal dung, with immense consequent damage to their environments. Nearly 1.5 billion people now burn wood to heat their homes and cook their food. The extent of the world firewood crisis and the measures being sought and taken against it are discussed in the forestry chapter of this book (chapter 9). Suffice it to add here that if the loss of soil through deforestation is not halted and reversed, the supply of food available to the rural poor will also sharply diminish.

The urgent environmental issue faced by energy planners in aid-giving and aid-receiving institutions is not, therefore, simply to minimize the environmental impact of large-scale power projects, although that task must not be ignored. It is also to make available environmentally benign forms of energy to those whose energy use now threatens to destroy their own environments.

Large-scale power projects will, of course, continue to be essential: a reduced rate of economic growth is utterly unacceptable to developing countries, whose commitment to increased energy production remains an urgent priority. Indeed, to avoid competition for scarce oil and to keep the staggering Third World external debt at a minimum, it is clearly in the interests of developed countries to promote energy self-sufficiency in the developing world. Thus, assistance may be provided in two new areas: for the exploitation of previously untapped fossil fuel reserves, and also for the development and widespread application of alternative energy sources which would be substitutes for either firewood or petroleum, or both.

The focus of this chapter cannot, however, embrace the world energy crisis as a whole. It must concentrate on the environmental implications of the energy policies encountered in nine multilateral aid institutions. Accordingly, discussion is restricted to three topics. First, the traditional energy lending which these agencies have favored is summarized and the typical measures used to assess and alleviate the environmental impact of those programs is briefly reviewed.

Second, the emerging energy strategies of the power divisions in the banks and technical assistance agencies visited, and the extent to which there is any awareness of the need for alternative or additional approaches are reviewed. Finally, this chapter considers the potential for policy changes in energy lending which would bring alternative energy supplies to the poor in rural areas.

Established Patterns of Lending

Almost all energy aid from the agencies that have been examined has been concentrated upon the commercial supply of high-grade (electrical) energy in large units designed to serve industrial plants and to provide for urban amenities. Excepting nuclear power plants (which have been exclusively financed through bilateral credits outside the sphere of development aid), the heavy energy lending of the World Bank and regional development banks to hydro schemes, oil- or gas-fired power stations, and other electrical energy projects represents about 20 percent of World Bank (IBRD) lending historically, 20 percent of the lending of the Inter-American Development Bank (IDB), 23 percent of the Asian Development Bank (AsDB), 22 percent in the case of the European Development Fund (EDF), and about the same proportion in the case of the African and Arab Development Banks.

The state of affairs reflected by the statistics shown in table 7-1 illustrates two conditions that have governed development strategies in the past and that still constrain them. The first, referred to elsewhere in this book, is the simplified assumption that equates Third World development largely with urban-based industrial expansion, and presumes that advance in this sector is the key to raising productivity. The second assumption, a corollary of this view, is that energy aid should focus on low unit cost centralized production of electricity and seek to develop energy systems and sources of supply most suited to this goal. Identification of energy development policies with national strategic interests and market forces blocks consideration of small-scale, installed, non-electric energy technologies in the aid transfer process.

It is quite clear that governmental priorities in the energy field, at least, have shown little if any sign of change from this pattern. Electric grid-based energy planning and lending enjoys an immense built-in momentum. Established interests, the relative ease and speed of project execution (it is *the* classic example of "transplant-development"), and the fact that once electric transmission systems are installed the rationale of extending them becomes almost overwhelming, combine to constrict innovative projects. These forces, in addition to the financial rate of return requirements of development banks, put major constraints on efforts to get energy supplies to the rural poor.

The patterns of energy lending of the institutions visited have quite naturally been reflected in the way these agencies have organized and staffed themselves to handle energy projects. These arrangements also help to block new lending approaches. The AsDB's Power Division, for example, has in its history funded only three nonelectric projects (all of them for natural gas transmission). The head of that division had heard of a village pilot project in Sri Lanka for solar and other alternative energy sources sponsored by the United Nations Environment Programme, but had not been able to learn anything about it.

The situation at the IDB is roughly similar, although there has always been a heavy emphasis on lending for large dams. (See chapter 8.) Only two people at the IDB had anything more than superficial knowledge about "income" energy technologies.

In the United Nations Development Programme (UNDP) and the Specialised Agencies which execute its projects, attempts to offer a balanced service of advice and technical help on energy have been overshadowed by the fact that the only institution in the whole U.N. "family" with exclusive energy responsibilities is the International Atomic Energy Agency (IAEA). (In recent years the IAEA has accounted for about 20 percent of UNDP funds devoted to energy related technical assistance.) According to a 1976 account of UNDP activities in the energy field,[1] its system of agencies sponsors a mass of small-scale, uncoordinated activities, mostly symposia, committees, technical consultancies, training seminars, and reporting functions. As a whole, however, they lacked (as Dr. Kurt Waldheim's recent proposal for the creation of an International Energy Institute suggested) any clear priority for training, research, or development of income energy technologies suited to the particular needs of poor countries without their own capital resources of coal, oil, or uranium.

The vast majority of energy projects at the World Bank are executed in the Electric Power Divisions of its six regional offices. However, as discussed below, it is clear that the World Bank is expanding its nonelectric energy lending and has therefore given considerable thought to the substantive implications of its energy organization.

Environmental Assessment of Traditional Power Projects

Some of the multilateral aid agencies have devoted considerable effort, in both staff time and consultancies, to assessing the environmental side effects of their energy lending. These assessments, although unquestionably valuable, have, as will be seen from the examples given here, examined environmental impact in the negative sense of simply avoiding adverse direct effects.

The IDB seems to have an increasingly impressive record in this area. Its work with the OAS, planning river basin development for power and other purposes, is discussed later, in chapter 8. Here, it should be noted that obvious environmental threats are at least considered. In the case of the Arenal

Table 7-1
Established Patterns of Lending

Agency (and valid date [fiscal year] for statistics):[a]

Type of Project[b]	*Number*	*Contribution (U.S. $ millions)*	*Total Percentage of Agency's Power/Energy*
World Bank (1972-1977)			
Power Generation			
Hydroelectric	22	$1,121.4	25.6%
Thermal	32	1,042.3	23.8%
Subtotal	54	2,163.7	49.4%
Transmission and Distribution			
Rural Electrification	4	132.0	3.0%
Other	31	1,719.7	39.2%
Fossil Fuel, Exploration			
and Recovery	2	298.0	6.8%
Geothermal	2	66.3	1.5%
Nuclear[c]	0	0.0	0.0%
Nonconventional[d]	2	1.2	0.039%
Totals	95	$4,380.9	100.0%
Inter-American Development Bank (1972-1976)			
Power Generation			
Hydroelectric[e]	15	$838.4	58.0%
Thermal	0	0.0	0.0%
Subtotal	15	838.4	58.0%
Transmission and Distribution			
Rural Electrification	6	123.3	8.5%
Other[f]	10	482.6	33.4%
Fossil Fuel Exploration			
and Recovery	0	0.0	0.0%
Geothermal[g]	0	0.0	0.0%
Nuclear	0	0.0	0.0%
Nonconventional	0	0.0	0.0%
Totals	31	$1,444.3	100.0%
Asian Development Bank (1972-1977)			
Power Generation			
Hydroelectric	20	$350.2	37.2%
Thermal	21	146.3	15.5%
Other	4	82.7	8.8%
Subtotal	45	579.2	61.5%
Transmission and Distribution[h]	25	349.8	37.2%
Fossil Fuel Exploration			
and Recovery	1	12.2	1.3%
Geothermal	0	0.0	0.0%
Nuclear	0	0.0	0.0%
Nonconventional	0	0.0	0.0%
Totals	71	$941.2	100.0%

Table 7-1 *continued*

Agency (and valid date [fiscal year] for statistics):[a]

Type of Project[b]	Number	Contribution (U.S. $ millions)	Total Percentage of Agency's Power/Energy
UNDP (as of June 30, 1976)			
Central Power Generation, Transmission and Distribution	31	$9.6	19.3%
Hydroelectric Power	12	8.5	17.2%
Grid-Related Power Projects			
Subtotal	43	18.1	36.5%
Energy Planning, etc.	9	3.1	6.3%
Hydrocarbon Fuels, (Exploration and Utilization Other than for Central Power)	40	15.9	32.0%
Geothermal	13	6.8	13.6%
Nuclear Power (Including Uranium Exploration)	24	5.6	11.4%
Nonconventional Energy Sources	7	.185	0.4%
Totals	136	$49.7	100.0%

[a]These statistics are compiled from the annual reports of each institution, with the exception of UNDP, which provided prepared statistical summaries, and from the research of Ms. Christine Howard of the U.S. Department of Energy, International Affairs Division. The tables for the IBRD, IDB, and AsDB are based on total energy lending over the stated period. The table for UNDP aid follows the accounting system used by that agency in its annually prepared *UNDP Compendium of Approved Projects*, which is to list all projects "that had been approved but not yet completed as of" a certain date; in this case, June 30, 1976.

[b]Frequently, projects include funding for generation (hydro or thermal) and transmission. These projects are included in the category that reflects the major component. The distinctions are rendered problematic in most cases by the fact that large power projects ordinarily involve sums much larger than the aid or loan, and concessional funds are therefore catalyzing the entire venture regardless of how they are formally allocated.

[c]The World Bank has not directly financed a nuclear project since a loan to Italy twenty years ago.

[d]The Ulla Ulla Rural Development Project was approved early in 1978 for a total of $18 million. It includes $120,000 for Bolivian research on solar cookers. A 1975 loan to Israel involves research on solar ponds and five "prime movers" (engines), which are being designed for use with a variety of nonconventional energy sources. These two components accounted for $1.1 million of a $35 million loan. Apparently, no project has yet been approved which includes an *operational* nonconventional energy component, although a few such projects are now being prepared.

[e]One project listed as hydroelectric also included a thermal generating component.

[f]Two of these projects are oil and gas pipelines, for which the IDB lent $123 million.

[g]The IDB is now willing to lend for geothermal energy and has one project in preparation.

[h]Includes two loans, totalling $65.4 million, for gas pipeline and distribution.

Hydroelectric project in Costa Rica approved in October 1974, for example, the IDB employed a volcanologist from the Smithsonian Institution to study and make recommendations concerning the threat from a major eruption of the nearby Arenal volcano. Following the environmental report, the design of the dam was substantially modified to reduce potential danger to the downstream area, although effects of the upstream catchment area on the dam unfortunately were not considered. The IDB also required establishment of a board of consultants, including experts in biology and hydrology, to deal with poisonous vegetation that was expected to grow in the reservoir area, and to analyze and make recommendations concerning the effects of discharging water from the reservoir on the Atlantic side of the country into the Santa Rosa River on the Pacific side of the country.[2]

The observation in chapter 3, that the IDB was not alert to incorporate its approved environmental requirements into its guidelines for feasibility study preparation in the power sector, must be reiterated. This has only been done as recently as September 1977, when new guidelines were issued in draft form.

The work of the Power Divisions at the World Bank has been monitored carefully by the Office of Environmental and Health Affairs (OEHA). When necessary, projects have been delayed pending modifications. This occurred in the case of a geothermal power project in El Salvador, where "extensive steps were taken to protect the Rio Paz and its riparian inhabitants from high levels of arsenic and boron."[3] In fact, this project illustrates one of the advantages of establishing clear environmental responsibilities. Interviews revealed that two World Bank supervision missions failed to report anything amiss with this project, which was under construction. An OEHA official had doubts, however, and personally traveled to El Salvador. Following this inspection and the discovery that pollution abatement design was being ignored, the OEHA successfully demanded that the project be brought into compliance with the design it had originally approved. Of particular interest here is the judgment of an OEHA official that if proper protective measures had been incorporated at the outset, the additional cost would have been $1.5 million; however, the subsequent additional work required to protect the riparian inhabitants added $12-13 million to project costs.

The Asian Development Bank (AsDB) has no formal environmental require-ments in the power sector, although it does appear to examine, on a purely informal basis, the environmental effects of selected power sector projects. In the case of the Mindanao Power Projects in the Philippines, the government expressed an interest in potential environmental impacts, which resulted in an environmental assessment and a limnological reconnaissance (of the affected Lake Lanao). In the case of the Asan Bay Power Project, the AsDB appears to have taken the initiative itself. The contractor was told to consider environmen-tal problems in determining the most appropriate fuel (oil or bituminous coal), and to consider environmental protection (which was not defined in further detail) in the design of the plant. Air pollution was the Bank's apparent concern, and it appears that the feasibility study assumed there would be no thermal pollution because of the use of sea water for once-through cooling.

If environmental issues seem significant to the project engineer, terms of reference for technical assistance and appraisal missions of the AsDB may, as a result, mention environmental parameters. There is no sector policy paper for the AsDB Power Division, although one is being prepared which will probably describe the Bank's energy strategy as encouraging the use of indigenous resources. At the very least, better dissemination of environmental information and some sort of in-house training program is needed at the AsDB. In many cases, professional environmental expertise is required, but unfortunately, in its absence, the lack of basic environmental information or data is often overlooked.

Current and Emerging Energy Strategies

Three developments—spiraling oil prices, a worldwide shortage of firewood, and the unfolding of a new strategy for development aid to the poorest—have caused aid agencies to begin to reconsider the limitations of traditional energy lending. Present indications are that some of the institutions studied intend to mount programs aimed at the new foreign exchange burden which high oil prices have strapped onto many developing countries. In fact, the World Bank now aims to lend $500 million per year spread over six to eight projects in the areas of oil, gas, and coal by 1980.

Until recently, the World Bank limited itself to an energy advisor working within its Department of Energy, Water, and Telecommunications. In December 1977, he became an assistant department director for Energy and Fuels, with a professional staff of ten. The bulk of electric power projects continue to be executed by the Regional Power Divisions, which seem largely insulated from any innovations that might emerge elsewhere in the Bank. However, an apparatus with the potential to coordinate wider energy strategies has now been created.

These broadened energy horizons at the World Bank should be welcomed from an environmental point of view. However, its new Energy and Fuels Department contains only one staff member working full-time on rural energy strategies and planning. If results continue to show promise, the Bank should perhaps establish a rural energy unit, just as it has set up a special team to develop its fossil fuels program. Finally, as will be discussed in detail below, instances of alternate energy planning have very recently begun to appear as components of urban and rural development projects.

The World Bank, the IDB, the UNDP, and the OAS have each given varying indications of being aware that "income" energy strategies may eventually play a role in their programs, but recent initiatives seem in no way commensurate with the scale of the problem, and, in particular, seem to overlook the need for comprehensive programs that discourage, rather than foster, long-run dependence on fossil fuels.[4] Nonconventional energy programs have been underemphasized and postponed in part because energy analyses have largely assumed that "demand" should be measured by industrial and commercial usage. However, especially in the case of fuelwood projects, there are encouraging signs at the World Bank of interest in noncommercial rural fuel supplies (see chapter 9).

The World Bank's 1975 study *India: The Energy Sector* acknowledged that "with respect to these dominant forms of fuel consumption in rural areas, there has so far been relatively little study, planning or concerted development."[5] In spite of this recognition, the five papers that had been commissioned prior to the final study concerned coal mining, the petroleum industry, the electric power industry, and the supply and demand of mining equipment and heavy electrical equipment.[6] Perhaps prior to completion of the study no one had noticed the gap in knowledge concerning rural energy, but that seems extremely unlikely, and only underlines the point. There has been no study either in the IDB, the World Bank, or any of the other institutions that were covered, that based energy analysis on a full understanding of *noncommercial* energy "demand" (there are prospects for such work in the World Bank regarding Colombia and perhaps Malawi); and yet, as long ago as 1971, it was estimated that noncommercial consumption as a percentage of total energy consumption was 45 percent in South America, 51 percent in Africa, and 58 percent in Asia.[7]

What, then, are the prospects for the future? In May 1977, the World Bank prepared a major policy study, *Minerals and Energy in the Developing Countries.* Its precise contents are restricted to internal Bank use, but its basic purpose was to argue for large new commitments by the World Bank (with the implicit hope that the regional banks would cooperate) in the field of oil, gas, and coal projects. In reaching this decision, the World Bank relied principally on its analysis that many developing countries, which are now net importers, could become self-sufficient for fossil fuels or even net exporters. The Bank's past neglect of alternate energy programs is scarcely surprising in light of its optimism that developing countries can produce enough fossil fuel to compete, economically, with the price of their imports (and which would not be absorbed by the world market), but this new commitment to indigenous fuels lending would make considerably greater sense and reach greater numbers of people if carried out in conjunction with an overall rural energy program.

The World Bank's position on financing nuclear power plants is based wholly on economic criteria. Given the rising costs and uncertainties connected with nuclear plants since the last Bank statement was made on nuclear power; given the unsuitability of the scale of reactors currently available to the energy needs of relatively small electric grids; given the escalation of already enormous unit costs involved; given also the concessional finance available for nuclear power from external aid sources (for example, the U.S. Export-Import Bank); it does not appear likely that the World Bank will become involved in lending for nuclear-generated electricity.

World Bank staff have pointed to several developments, still primarily at the theoretical level, that seem likely to result in a more diversified World Bank energy strategy. In its formal statement to the panel on "International Cooperation in Energy" of the Tenth World Energy Conference, held in Istanbul, September 19-23, 1977, the Bank announced "a rural energy program . . . to develop guidelines and strategies for rural energy planning in developing countries." It listed four ongoing activities of this program:

1. A study of the overall rural energy demand and supply situation, in various countries and regions, to provide a basis for rural energy policies.
2. Development of a rural energy planning approach for translating rural energy policies into projects or project components that will include the least-cost mix of various renewable and nonrenewable energy resources for meeting energy demand for subsistence and development.
3. Experimentation with rural energy components in regular Bank forestry, rural development, or other rural sector projects.
4. Investigation into rural energy technologies that could be applied in developing countries for their rural areas.[8]

So far this program has produced an effort to develop alternate energy strategies for rural energy planning and development in Colombia, to which a considerable commitment of staff time has been given. This work is discussed in greater detail later in this chapter. With spreading recognition of the firewood crisis, the World Bank is also planning a major expansion of lending for biomass energy in the form of fuelwood projects. This approach is both direct in dealing with the needs of the poorest, and environmentally sound in that it helps restore depleted soils and ravaged forest areas denuded of trees by the search for fuel.

The World Bank has attempted to encourage a certain amount of research. It recently commissioned a study of the potential for utilization of solar power and other energy resources in northeast Brazil, and several years ago, the Bank's Office of the Science Advisor sponsored research into the potential for biogas and solar energy in less-developed countries.[9]

The IDB continues to focus more narrowly than the World Bank in the energy field. A senior IDB energy official explained that neither the IDB nor Latin American governments can afford politically to concentrate on the rural poor because of the overwhelming problems presented by migration to the cities over the last fifteen years.[10] Consequently, the IDB's energy strategy will look no further, for the foreseeable future, than to an expansion into oil and gas projects with some room for funding geothermal power projects. These, at least, are the plans outlined in "Latin American Energy and Oil: Present Situation and Prospects."[11] This paper is now being revised as the basis for an IDB energy policy which has been requested by its Board of Directors.

The IDB appears to take the view that transformation away from an oil-based economy will depend, for developing countries, on three factors: energy conservation and fuel substitution by developed countries; development in the industrialized countries of new energy sources that can be transferred successfully to other areas of the world; and increased access for less-developed countries to large amounts of financial and technical resources that will sustain economic growth. In short, the IDB view is that developing countries cannot afford the risks of innovation but will develop future energy strategies only in light of similar, antecedent commitments made by the developed countries.

Officials of the IDB said that they can only consider projects that involve commercially proven technology, and most alternate energy proposals are therefore "out of the question" for the time being. This restriction may have to be lifted by the IDB's Board of Directors, however, if they decide to establish a program of lending to catalyze private investment in fossil fuel exploration and recovery. The IDB should also be urged to modify the restriction in the case of nonconventional energy projects, particularly since the foreign exchange requirement of such projects is often quite small and they could frequently be carried out under the technical assistance activities of the IDB. For the time being, the only exception to this general IDB rule has been exploration for geothermal energy potential in Costa Rica, where $500,000 was granted in the form of technical cooperation on a contingent recovery basis.

So far as longer-range policies are concerned, the IDB has informally endorsed the probability expressed in *Energy for Rural Development*,[12] that "a decade or two must pass before any of what are now regarded as promising unconventional energy sources will assume a significant role in the energy supply picture . . . promising sources do not match well with the demands of energy users in developing nations." However, as has been noted, "demands of energy users" conceptually exclude the needs of much of the world's population.

Thus, it may be true, given the *present* state of political determination and institutional commitment, that a decade or two will indeed pass before alternate energy sources are widely available. But to a degree it is also tautological. The conclusion begs the question whether developing countries, the majority of those who live in them, and the institutions that seek to serve their needs, can afford to wait these twenty years in the hope that the desperate needs of so many people—and of their environments—can be monetized into effective commercial energy demand.

Neither the UNDP nor the OAS has yet formulated an energy strategy. Given the remarkably small proportion of UNDP resources allocated to energy, it would make little sense for that organization to follow the oil/gas commitment of the large banks (although it has funded some exploration). At least in the *absence* of a strategy that discounts alternative energy possibilities, opportunities in this area could perhaps be pushed quickly to the fore. This may happen, for example, as the result of a request from the United Nations Economic and Social Council that UNEP and UNDP be receptive to requests from developing countries for support to develop alternative energy sources.[13] To stimulate thoughtful project requests, an "Interagency Group on Alternative Energy Sources in Latin America" was convened in Mexico City early in 1977. It recommended two studies now being implemented, one to identify energy requirements in Latin America that might be met with alternate technologies, and the other to survey the region's existing ability to apply these technologies. The UNDP project document comments that "The Preparatory Assistance addresses itself to the use of renewable energy resources, and therefore has a positive environmental impact."

The UNDP's Technical Advisory Division (TAD) has several staff members who are aware of the potential of nonconventional energy sources, but little thought has been given to the energy implications of policies in related fields. For example, the drafters of the 1978 TAD Management Plan in Rural Development had not, prior to this study, planned to include any discussion of rural energy needs (which might have been particularly appropriate since these policy papers are *not* limited to a review of current activities).

It would be premature to hope that the UNDP could spearhead alternate energy work within the U.N. system. It lacks funds for such a task, and, in any event, is required to respond to the diverse, often inconsistent requests of governments for energy assistance. But a commitment to encourage the establishment of many such programs could be the cornerstone of an alternate energy strategy for some countries or regions, which, with effective management (for example, of biomass programs), would be lower in environmental impact and of greater sustainability than conventional hydro, gas, or fossil fuel sources.

The OAS reflects the wishes and policies of member governments at least as much as any institution included in this study. In the energy field, its Program of Regional Development has worked on hydropower projects (in the prefeasibility stage), while its Department of Scientific Affairs has taken the lead in encouraging the development of new technologies. In later 1976, the OAS sponsored a widely attended "Seminar on Development of Non-Conventional Energy Sources" at the University of the West Indies in Trinidad and Tobago. Dr. Marcelo Alonso, Director of the Department of Scientific Affairs, gave the keynote address, in which he said:

> No . . . breakthrough for high density energy production is in sight in the near future to alleviate our critical dependence on fossil fuels, especially oil and gas, except for nuclear energy, which has already come of age, and its increased use in the forthcoming decades is inevitable and absolutely necessary. This is the real incentive for renewed and intensive research on new forms of energy production, and

for setting up stringent measures for energy conservation. *On the other hand, there is a distinct possibility of achieving in the next decade or two effective new energy sources for rural areas.* [Emphasis added.]

Dr. Alonso, who has recently reactivated the Inter-American Nuclear Energy Commission, also went on to consider in detail the possible applications in Latin America of alternate energy sources.

The past year has confirmed and deepened the dual commitment of the OAS to emphasize nuclear and nonconventional energy, particularly solar. A recent OAS paper concluded that "It is necessary to increase substantially the funds dedicated to research and development in solar energy. Only in one country (Brazil) does adequate funding exist for this purpose, specifically for direct utilization of solar energy and for biomass production of alcohol."[14] Of greater importance, the OAS has backed its policies with its money by funding a "Special Project on Utilization of Solar Energy." It remains to be seen how far the OAS commitment to renewable energy resources will be carried, but it could prove to be quite important if it were to catalyze coordinated action by the other agencies active in Latin America.

To sum up the recent policy initiatives in the banks and technical assistance agencies, it seems that some of the larger institutions have begun to reconsider their energy lending policies primarily in light of the ending of cheap oil with rather less emphasis on the depletion of firewood supplies and new strategies to meet basic human needs. Their reactions so far have been to concentrate on helping countries find new indigenous fossil fuel or gas reserves.

The World Bank and the regional banks have done much less, however, in encouraging pilot project work using other (especially solar) technologies. A few of these technologies appear to be commercially and economically feasible at the present time (particularly small-scale hydroelectric stations), but this is primarily an area of urgent need for research, institution building, and experimental work, especially in Asia and Africa. In Latin America, rural institutions are often more sophisticated and may be better able to cope with organizing pilot and experimental solar and other technologies.

Encouraging Prospects: Toward a Rural
Energy Strategy

None of the specific policy initiatives that were located offer much institutional encouragement for the development of renewable energy resources. This becomes increasingly worrisome in view of the fate of Dr. Kurt Waldheim's proposal for the creation of an International Energy Institute.[15] A few alternate energy projects have nevertheless emerged from the multilateral aid institutions, and in one or two cases alternate energy planning has been incorporated into larger projects. Some of these merit closer attention.

As of June 30, 1977, the UNDP had funded eleven projects that used various forms of alternate energy technology, at a total cost to UNDP of $888,335. One of these was a charcoal production project which cost $630,956; the other ten were all small research components in larger projects, receiving an average of roughly $25,000 of UNDP funds. A more ambitious undertaking formulated several years ago in cooperation with the Economic and Social Commission for Asia and the Pacific (ESCAP) had to be abandoned at that time for lack of funds, but is being revived. This project, designed to assemble and support a rural energy task force for the ESCAP region, would include a UNDP contribution toward technical assistance for new technologies (wind, biogas, solar, and small-scale hydroelectric), and would also allow for seminars, expert exchanges, and pilot projects funded by the participating governments.

From all indications, the UNDP wants to respond eagerly to Colombian initiatives to expand and publicize "Las Gaviotas," a rural development center in the sparsely populated Llanos area. Six inexpensive devices have been designed there, which provide water and electricity and save considerable amounts of human labor. The Dutch aid agency and the UNDP will jointly fund a factory to manufacture these units in quantity. In addition, the most recent country program for Ecuador includes a funding request for a project modeled on "Las Gaviotas," and the World Bank is providing $250,000 toward the establishment of a similar rural service center for the Amazon region of Colombia.

Like the UNDP, the OAS may be able to stimulate interest and action out of proportion to its rather limited funds. It has established a "Special Project on Utilization of Solar Energy" in which Argentina, Brazil, Jamaica, Mexico, and Trinidad and Tobago have all participated. The project involves "research and development in solarimetry and in the . . . utilization of solar energy . . . [and] development of indigenous technology and expertise in solar energy utilization . . . [and] training of engineers, scientists and technicians."[16] Through 1977, the project has been allocated $540,000 of OAS funds, a substantial percentage of OAS resources. The content of each country's programs is left to its own judgment, and there is therefore a wide range of components (not all of which seem especially well suited to the circumstances). But the concept of the project, locally directed research oriented toward known local needs, is one that should be endorsed and emulated.

Among the regional development banks, the AsDB's only activity has been, very recently, to include in the terms of reference for an integrated rural development project for Nepal the requirement that there be a "determination of the potentiality of hydropower and biogas plants" as rural power sources.

The World Bank's Board of Directors very recently approved $165,000 in technical assistance to support preexisting Bolivian research on solar energy, as part of the $18 million Ulla Ulla Rural Development Project. This is the first *approved* World Bank project to include any support for local research on nonconventional energy technology. The Bank anticipates three years of research, by which time a second phase Ulla Ulla project could finance local costs for solar cookers and heaters.

The World Bank recognized that the wide range of innovations included in Ulla Ulla necessarily implies a high degree of administrative risk, and the Board's approval assumed that modifications would perhaps be necessary during project implementation. If the World Bank, or any agency, wishes to encourage innovative work in the energy field (or in any area that places a premium on local initiative and innovation), it places an added burden on staff. Innovative projects consume additional staff time, but this fact must be recognized and accepted in the energy sector (as indeed it frequently has been in other areas).

A livestock project in Mali which was approved in 1974 seems unique in the way that it combines grounds both for optimism and discouragement. In this case, World Bank staff have searched unsuccessfully for a renewable energy source to power pumps for waterholes. Wind power, solar power, mechanically transposed animal traction, and human pedal pumps were all considered. The solar option was economically feasible but the only company that could produce the needed product was not prepared to oversee a large operation in the Sahel. Until an appropriate alternate energy source is designed or located, comparatively costly wells are being dug in lieu of waterholes. The Bank staff's encouraging determination to search for a locally appropriate, feasible energy technology dramatizes the need for a larger and more comprehensive commitment to research and develop those technologies. Given the scant organized attention that has been paid to the energy requirements of this type of project, it is hardly surprising that no solution has yet been found. And yet, it would be difficult to imagine a project more clearly designed to meet some of the basic needs of a rural population in one of the world's most bedeviled areas.[17]

There are more such projects at various stages of gestation in the World Bank, which may include small components of locally appropriate energy planning because an alert staff member seized an opportunity. But the Bank has moved extremely cautiously to undertake projects whose *primary* purpose would be to develop renewable energy sources. One such project carried out in Israel has already been mentioned.[18] One of the justifications for this project was "the potential benefits of a successful outcome in a world with increasing energy needs."

A rural energy planning program has been devised with World Bank assistance by the Colombian government, which has organized a Rural Energy Group to study the relationship between energy and rural development. This has been carried out by conducting extensive surveys of farmers in a case study region. Now the Colombians will try to identify pilot projects for World Bank funding, using the least-cost mix for indigenous, primarily nonconventional energy sources.

The World Bank's experiences in Colombia, even though no particular project has yet been identified, have uncovered some serious obstacles. Although

Colombia's mountainous areas suffer from serious deforestation, government planners at first refused to believe that a "rural energy problem" existed. Colombia is recognized as having a rather innovative national development program, and yet it had no institutional capability of any kind for addressing its rural energy shortage. Thus, everything in this program has had to be organized from scratch.

However, the vacuum into which the World Bank and the Colombian Rural Energy Group have stepped may prove a strength of this program. There is no alternative to talking to villagers, identifying their needs, and planning accordingly. Local fuel supplies will be identified. The need for electricity will be pinpointed rather than assumed, and research will be initiated to adapt or develop low cost and nonelectric technologies. In short, a process rather than a technology has been the principal focus of the effort. It is far too early to anticipate, let alone judge, results. But an approach to rural energy needs, and the quality of life which relies on meeting those needs, is being developed. Its potential seems worthy of remark.

In general, it seemed that the occurrence of nonconventional energy projects, or of such energy components in larger projects, usually results from individual staff interest or initiative. The two exceptions to this are work done by the OAS and the UNDP, which in the latter case, at least, has remained a tiny fraction of its overall energy funding, and the Colombian rural energy initiative taken by the World Bank, which presumably represents the first small step on the rural energy road promised in Istanbul.

Conclusions and Recommendations

There are a few encouraging signs in the search for innovative energy projects that seek to improve the condition of the rural poor with minimal impact on their environment. First is the recent attention given by the World Bank (discussed in chapter 9) to fuelwood projects. Next, there seems to be a restless awareness among staff at many of the institutions visited that a problem looms whose dimensions have not yet been appraised, and for which no solutions of adequate scale have been brought forward. Against this must be measured the insistence of advocates of large-scale power projects that the usefulness of alternate energy technologies is overestimated for the foreseeable future. Since the proponents of this view control very substantial sums of money allocated for energy lending, their arguments tend to be self-confirming.

A third encouraging trend is the belief, apparently widespread, that funds for local research and institution building may be an important means of meeting rural energy needs. This approach has spillover advantages: it can create jobs in research, local construction, and marketing (for example at "Las Gaviotas"), and thereby can boost the productivity of an area. A second advantage, as the World Bank's *Appropriate Technology in World Bank Activities* has wisely pointed out, is that demonstration projects are frequently ineffective unless supported by a local organization and executed on a large enough scale under typical circumstances. An important objective of rural energy lending programs should, be, therefore, to instigate local activity and action.

The environmental value of linking rural energy lending to a program aimed at meeting basic needs may be understood by a few, but it has not received attention or funding on anywhere near the scale needed to have even a small impact on the lives of the many hundreds of millions of people who damage their environments in their reliance on dwindling noncommercial energy sources. In this context, it may be that the large resource implications of a rush to develop oil and gas reserves have not been adequately examined. In particular, fossil fuel dependency is being encouraged at a time when it may turn out to be no more than a short-run strategy. Admittedly, the foreign exchange burden faced by developing countries as a result of the oil price increases is a critical constraint. But planning for the next ten to fifteen years should proceed simultaneously and in harmony with longer-term energy planning.

It might seem premature or presumptuous to make specific recommendations to institutions about the solution of a problem which many of them have not conceded is their proper concern. But some specific suggestions do readily present themselves.

1. The UNDP and the OAS are ideally situated to play a significant role and to galvanize action in development banks whose funds are badly needed. This may be particularly important for Latin America. There the appearance of action may be deceiving, since the intensive effort to develop oil and gas reserves may mean that rural energy needs are in grave danger of being ignored altogether.

2. Planning and analysis should be focused on energy demand as a whole, not simply on demand for electric power generation. At the World Bank this may mean that the creation at some point of an overall energy policy would eventually result in a reorientation of the Regional Power Divisions. However, it is probably preferable to concentrate small-scale energy planning in the divisions that work with rural—or urban—beneficiaries, and provide them with the support of a rural energy team, as previously suggested. There is of course the danger, so long as alternate energy planning remains a sporadic element of rural or urban projects, that neither staff nor funds will be committed systematically and on the requisite scale. Other institutions studied have not even begun to address alternative, renewable energy questions.

3. The Tenth World Energy Conference in Istanbul resolved that the eleventh conference, to be held in Hamburg in 1980, will have as its main theme the "energy problems of the developing countries." This meeting could become a valuable focus of attention for planners and management in aid institutions. In

the absence of an International Energy Institute, this may prove a vital forum in which necessary commitment can be stimulated.

Notes

1. United Nations Economic and Social Council (ECOSOC) Document E/C7/47/Add 3, 24 February 1975.

2. Testimony of C. Fred Bergsten, Assistant Secretary for International Affairs of the U.S. Department of Treasury, *Hearings before the Subcommittee on Foreign Operations* and *Related Agencies of the Committee on Appropriations*, U.S. House of Representatives, 95th Congress, First Session, Part One, p. 521.

3. Ibid., p. 176.

4. It has been pointed out that "the dwindling of world petroleum reserves and the depletion of woodlands reinforce each other; climbing firewood prices encourage more people to use petroleum-based products for fuel, while soaring oil prices make this shift less feasible, adding to the pressure on forests." Erik Eckholm, *The Other Energy Crisis: Firewood*, Worldwatch Paper no. 1. (Washington, D.C., September 1975), pp. 17-18.

5. P.D. Henderson, *India: The Energy Sector* (Washington, D.C., International Bank for Reconstruction and Development, 1975), p. 166.

6. Ibid., p. 3.

7. Darmstadter, Joel, *Energy in the World Economy*, 1971. More recent studies have reaffirmed this picture. See *Energy Needs, Uses and Resources in Developing Countries*, March 1978 (Washington, D.C., U.S. Agency for International Development Contract Study), figure C-1, p. 68.

8. *Proceedings of the Tenth World Energy Conference*, Statement of the IBRD presented to the Conference Panel on International Cooperation in Energy.

9. Two papers were prepared in November 1976, including "Critical Factors in Economic Evaluation of Small Decentralized Energy Projects," and "Solar Photovoltaic Cells in Developing Countries." The Bank's science advisor presented a third paper to a U.S. Energy, Research and Development Administration (ERDA) panel in January 1976 on "Developing Country Applications of Photovoltaic Cells."

10. Table 2, p. 391 of *Economic and Social Progress in Latin America*, shows that the urban population of Latin America rose from under 50.0 percent in 1960 to 62.3 percent in 1976. Inter-American Development Bank, 1976.

11. Paper presented to the Workshop on Energy Demand sponsored in Paris by the International Energy Agency in November 1977. The paper is not yet publicly available but was summarized in the February 1978 issue of *IDB News*.

12. U.S. National Academy of Sciences, *Energy for Rural Development:*

Renewable Resources and Alternative Technologies for Developing Countries (Washington, D.C., 1976), p. 5. (Reprinted with permission.) The argument in question was favorably received in *Promotion of Education, Science and Technology by the Energy Sector,* November 1976, by Ismael Escobar, Head of the Education, Science and Technology Section of the IDB's Project Analysis Department, pp. 22-24.

13. See Resolution 2031 (LXI), *Research and Development in Non-conventional Sources of Energy*, of the Economic and Social Council of the United Nations, 61st Session, August 4, 1976.

14. Marcelo Alonso and Miguel de Santiago, *Solar Energy in Latin America, An Overview* (Paper presented to the International Solar Energy Conference, New Delhi, January 16-21, 1978, p. 10). Reprinted with permission.

15. The International Energy Institute proposal seems most unlikely to gain the broad governmental support that would give it some chance of success, although it has attracted World Bank support.

16. See "Solar Energy in Latin America" and annexes, *supra.*

17. Another project which was very successful in locating a range of economically feasible applications of commercially available solar technology, and which would have slowed deforestation in one of the world's critically threatened areas, has been delayed, probably fatally, by the host government's preference for other projects. The World Bank has also moved ahead with a biogas component for the Second Calcultta Urban Project, a $180 million project to upgrade a large area of Calcutta. One site and service scheme includes $250,000 to build a biogas-powered sanitation system.

18. See footnote d, p. 81.

8 Water Resources

Water connects the activities of every community as vitally as does the bloodstream in a living body. Apart from its use for drinking, cooking, and washing, it is essential for the growing of food and for almost every industrial process and offers immense potential for producing electric energy.

Multilateral lending institutions have made water management a major focus of their lending programs. Water supply and sewer systems are found among the first loans of institutions such as the World Bank and the Inter-American Development Bank (IDB). Dams and irrigation systems are also found among the early loans of these banks and have been increasing in importance in recent years.

Like the established patterns of lending for large-scale energy projects which were discussed in the previous chapter, the efforts of multilateral aid institutions in the area of water resources have until quite recently reflected assumptions about growth and development that are now increasingly questioned. Lending activity has concentrated in three areas: the construction of hydroelectric dams, the creation of irrigation systems, and, to a lesser extent, the provision of water supplies primarily to urban areas.

In the case of dams and irrigation systems, secondary impacts and long-term sustainability of projects have often been overlooked. Urban water supply projects have taken precedence over rural water supply and over waste disposal for city and country alike.

Although it is true that world water supplies cannot run out, their allocation and distribution to people in safely usable condition is one of the few concerns truly indispensable to the maintenance of a livable, healthy human environment. Thus, like no other area of aid activity examined in this book, the development of water resources illustrates the dependence of the process of "development" on its natural environmental setting. Any development authority, be it a national ministry or an external assistance organization, cannot effectively provide basic human needs without considering the broad environmental implications of its water resource programs. These are discussed under three subdivisions: dams, irrigation, and water supply and waste disposal.

Dams, Irrigation, and Drainage Works

Dams, irrigation systems, and drainage works all involve major changes in the physical environment to achieve certain development objectives. Irrigating land

95

for better crops and providing electricity for use in cities, towns, and for industry are among the evident benefits of dams and irrigation projects. At the same time, possible increase and threat of diseases, increasing salinity and waterlogging from poorly managed irrigation projects, the destruction of delicate ecosystems, forced movement of local populations, and the elimination of wildlife and plant species must be weighed among the costs of these activities. The construction of dams frequently introduces changed living patterns for people relocated away from newly flooded areas, while bringing others in to work newly irrigated land.

Dams

Multilateral lending institutions have been increasing their financing of dams for production of hydroelectric power. In 1974, while the total installed hydropower capacity was well developed in the industrialized part of the world, "developing nations had installed less than 10 percent of their (potential) hydroelectric power generating capacity."[1]

With the increase in oil prices since 1973, hydropower is once again looked to as an economic way to produce electricity. Although in the early 1970s a cost of $300 to $400 per installed kilowatt of generating capacity was considered the limit, in 1976 and 1977, projects costing more than $1,000 per installed kilowatt were financed. For example, in Guatelama the 300,000 kilowatt project on the Chixoy River will cost $340.8 million. Except for a 120-kilometer transmission line, the entire cost is related to generation.

In recent years the World Bank (IBRD) has lent an annual average of $225 million for hydroelectric projects, the IDB $170 million, and the Asian Development Bank (AsDB) about $60 million.[2] The number of World Bank-financed hydropower projects has not sharply increased since 1975, but the total project funds of which the Bank forms a share has almost doubled.[3] Bank financial participation may be only 20 percent of the total project cost in a dam and hydropower installation. Since many borrowers count on the World Bank for future loans to expand their energy systems, and since the Bank's dollars generate the security needed for private banks to participate, its influence in insisting on good environmental practices can be generally much greater than its share of any particular consortium of financiers would suggest. Thus, recent trends in World Bank lending may mean that it can exert an increased qualitative influence without lending more money.

There are new opportunities to avoid the environmental mistakes of the past in the construction of large dams. Unfortunately, the relative cheapness of hydroelectric power has led to single purpose dams, the planning of which has tended to ignore, or treat in a perfunctory way, questions about resettlement, agriculture, fisheries in the reservoirs and downstream of the dams, changes in river flow, water quality, navigation, management of upper catchments, effect of forestry activities, and human health problems arising from water-related diseases.

The environmental impacts of large dams represent for the most part easily quantified adverse or beneficial effects associated with their construction and operation. But these effects are often ignored because they are not directly involved with the business of generating and transmitting electrical power. The obvious remedy is to manage dams for multiple purposes. This is problematic, however, because they are usually designed and financed as integral components of national energy systems, which, in turn, are usually run by semiautonomous power utilities who may be the borrowers. And these borrowers usually finance their loans on the basis of energy sales to large customers in urban industrial centers. Here at once there is a fundamental conflict. Whereas environmental effects are for the most part local (with the very important exception of the downstream effects on coastal and estuarine areas) the benefits of cheap, reliable power are enjoyed far away from the areas of environmental damage, and by people with the resources to raise the loans.

Moreover, feasibility studies for hydroelectric projects generally evaluate the least cost solution to electrical energy production, usually for a national market, rather than the overall economic costs and benefits of the project. Further, economic analysis is virtually a financial analysis in hydroelectric power projects, since the revenue-producing potential is the fundamental measure of project benefits. Since the costs and benefits of changes in fisheries, flood plain land use, erosion control, navigation, and health conditions are regional or local and more easily measured in social and economic terms, they are virtually precluded from a significant place in the feasibility level analysis of hydroelectric power projects. Only resettlement costs are routinely included in the analysis, and they tend to be underestimated.

What have the lending agencies done, or attempted to do to adjust this order of priorities? The World Bank's Environmental Handbook guides preparation of dam and irrigation projects in the World Bank. The Central Projects Staff responsible for this type of project have developed their own guidelines which seem to cover all aspects of feasibility studies except, apparently, environmental ones.

Environmentally related questions in the Bank's 1974 Handbook for the most part elicit "yes" or "no" answers (for example, "Will runoff water contain residues, such as pesticides and fertilizers, that contaminate downstream waters?"). They help to identify potential problems, but no guidance is provided in the Handbook for surveying these problems or, once they are measured, for evaluating them in the context of the project. Any revision of the guidelines should provide a methodology for evaluating the effects of the project on the environment.

At the World Bank, preliminary ecological surveys of dam projects are commissioned when a substantial environmental impact is foreseen. The Bank prefers that the borrower contract and pay for this work. The Bank's environmental officers consult the staff involved and provide general terms of reference for ecological studies of hydroelectric power schemes. The environmental staff may also review existing information on the project and develop terms of reference suited to the particular case. The results of the ecological surveys are always summarized in the final appraisal documents, and frequently the recommendations for remedial action become conditions of the loan agreement.

If a project is considered by the environmental staff to create unacceptable impacts, it may be held up even after final appraisal. In the case of the Sobradinho Dam on the Sao Francisco River in Brazil, the World Bank's ecological reconnaissance followed the loan and did not begin until after construction started. The results of the survey, including provisions for resettlement, schistosomiasis and malaria control, and review of downstream effects were added to the loan agreement and substantially implemented.

In the IDB, hydroelectric projects are prepared in the Infrastructure Division of the Project Analysis Department. The basic approach has been to let the borrower (generally the power utility company) establish what environmental impacts, if any, will be studied and ameliorated. This means in practice that some form of compensation and resettlement is usually provided for peoples and towns flooded by the dam, and included in the project cost. Fisheries, recreation, catchment, and other watershed management have usually been neglected, however. If complex environmental and other issues of concern to the borrower are posed, the IDB suggests a panel of consultants be formed to study and follow up on the issues during the project implementation. This approach was followed in the Arenal hydropower project in Costa Rica (see chapter 7).

It is the IDB's policy to insist that long-range master plans for electrical energy development be prepared and used to develop the least cost solution for projects which the IDB would finance.[4] Although not noted in the policy paper, it should be possible to employ environmental criteria at stages of analysis prior to the feasibility studies which justify loan requests. These studies occur at a stage of project development which, in the case of many environmental impacts, is too advanced to allow introduction of the mitigating measures.

IDB's latest electric energy sectoral *Guidelines* (dated September 1977) stipulate that hydroelectric projects should include a description of the impacts of the project's construction on local fauna and flora, landscape, the river course and geology, including areas below the dam, and on "cultural and economic values of the region." These guidelines are too new to have been tested.

The Program for Regional Development (PRD) of the Organization of American States (OAS) has for more than ten years helped Latin American nations in regional and river basin development studies, from the reconnaissance to the prefeasibility level. Although considerations of soil erosion, forest conservation, and watershed management had been included in these studies, the concern for the environment developing after 1972 and the Stockholm Conference presented special conceptual and methodological problems for river basin studies. As noted previously, it is not clear how or whether this work feeds into the practice of the banks themselves.

An OAS draft report of a pilot study identifies the kind of work of an environmental nature that can be done at different phases in prefeasibility level integrated studies, and suggests a format for analyzing impacts and for their evaluation.[5] Even though it is still a draft, it has influenced subsequent surveys conducted by the OAS in the Plate River system, namely in the Pilcomayo Basin and the Upper Paraguay River Basin. A significant improvement in these integrated studies resulting from the pilot experience is the addition of fisheries and limnological studies.

Further, terms of reference for negotiating an "environmental objective" are now being provided by the OAS to appraisal mission teams that develop requests for technical assistance into detailed work plans that later become the basis for agreements between the OAS and national governments. Although the new terms of reference have not yet been formalized, the procedure has been used already by appraisal missions to the Dominican Republic's Cibao region and to Brazil's Sao Francisco Valley, where the team was asked to pay special attention to the problems of the spread of schistosomiasis in a ground-water resource survey program.

In recent years, special watershed management projects have been undertaken by the United Nations Development Progamme (UNDP)—upper Solo watershed, Indonesia; Mae Sa watershed, Thailand; and Phewa Tal watershed, Nepal. These are characterized as integrated rural development programs which pursue the interdependent aims of run-off control, forestry, and rural development assistance. They do not specifically mention environmental effects.

Important contributions made by the UNDP towards the mitigation or management of environmental aspects of water resource development have included its pilot projects in water and soil management, designed to test improved "farm level" techniques of irrigation and crop husbandry, and its environmental review of the Jonglei Canal project in the Sudan. However, the hydrological impact of dams on the natural regimes of rivers and estuaries and the consequent and incremental effect on the fishes and other aquatic life are not yet being adequately treated in UNDP-financed hydroelectric power surveys.

Irrigation and Drainage Works

Lending by the World Bank and the International Development Association (IDA) in irrigation projects has increased dramatically in recent years. According to the annual reports of the World Bank, the total costs of irrigation projects, in which an average of 50 percent is covered by World Bank or IDA loans, was $813 million in 1975, $2,276 million in 1976 and $2,405 million in 1977. The Inter-American Development Bank (IDB) has lent over $800 million for irrigation in Latin America, most of it in Mexico. The AsDB has funded irrigation projects since 1969 (its first was the Tajun Project in Indonesia).

Irrigated lands are currently estimated at 200 million hectares worldwide, or 13 percent of the total cultivated area.[6] About half (95 million) of these irrigated hectares are adversely affected by salinity or alkalinity as a consequence of poor drainage. The U.N. Environment Programme (UNEP) estimates that each year an additional 200,000 to 300,000 hectares (2-3 percent) of presently irrigated land are lost because of waterlogging or salinization.[7] Thus, a considerable part of development financing for irrigated agriculture is required for environmental rehabilitation and renovation of existing systems. For example, since 1970, the World Bank and IDA have financed four separate drainage projects in Egypt to drain almost 1.25 million hectares.

The development of further schemes are relatively more costly, since the most attractive possibilities are already developed. An estimated $25 billion would be needed by 1985 to rehabilitate 50 million hectares. To bring an additional 25 million hectares under irrigation would cost approximately $40 billion (at 1975 prices).

The deterioration of upper catchments also tends to debilitate irrigation projects. Flooding and siltation of irrigation systems (as in Pakistan) has resulted from failure to consider the effects of deforestation on these projects. Schemes for rehabilitation should be accompanied by adequate environmental study and a major effort to build up effective management institutions. Some of these defects in irrigation projects increasingly are being remedied through the adoption of policies concerning the more equitable distribution of development benefits and the protection of the environment.

In the irrigation systems section of the World Bank's Environmental Handbook, no reference is made to potential pesticide dangers to fish and other aquatic biota, nor is schistosomiasis mentioned. Yet, these problems are serious and widespread. Moreover, like the dam section, the irrigation section does not explain or summarize the kinds of environmental impacts that can be expected in these projects.

Irrigation projects present a workable economic framework for incorporating environmental costs and benefits. However, in the *Guideline for the Preparation of Feasibility Studies for Irrigation and Drainage Projects*, used by the World Bank as well as by Food and Agriculture Organization (FAO) staff in the FAO/IBRD Cooperative Program,[8] there is no mention of environmental impacts such as alteration of water quality, or analysis of external diseconomies possibly associated with environmental impacts. Nor is reference made to the World Bank's Environmental Handbook. The purpose of the above-mentioned guideline was to describe a format for potential borrowers to show desired scope and content of feasibility studies in support of loan requests, and offers an opportunity to raise environmental questions in the earliest stages of project planning.

Also, despite the well-known, long-term global damage caused by chlorinated hydrocarbon pesticides (DDT, aldrin, dieldrin, and others), and the fact that they have been banned in many industrialized countries, their potential impacts are not routinely evaluated in irrigation project feasibility or prefeasibility surveys. The use of such chemicals for pest control is assumed in irrigated agricultural projects and the appropriateness of such use is not evaluated.[9]

As far as the International Institute for Environment and Development (IIED) team could determine, soil erosion control programs have rarely if ever been called for as part of irrigation (or dam) projects. However, several projects financed by the agencies reviewed have been badly affected because of serious (and generally at least partially manageable) erosion problems. Early World Bank dam projects in El Salvador and Tunisia and IDB dam and irrigation projects in Mexico were mentioned by those interviewed as being in this category. Environmental impacts are mentioned in another FAO publication, which simply states that:

> Some international financing institutions, including the World Bank, now seek explicit assurances that the project will have no adverse environmental effects before agreeing to pursue it. If significant environmental impact is likely, full treatment in an annex (of the feasibility study) is called for; otherwise a short explanatory paragraph will suffice.[10]

The World Bank's guidelines are not referenced for further explanation.

The guidelines for preparing loan requests to the IDB for agricultural development through water control, that is, irrigation, drainage, and storage (November 1977), include a lengthy appendix on the environmental aspects of such projects, entitled *Criterios Para Medir el Impacto de los Proyectos en el Medio Ambiente.* This appendix contains a most comprehensive and coherent treatment of environmental aspects and closely follows the World Bank's guidelines, including the use of a check list, but the IDB's list is more extensive. Its stated objectives are:

1. To prevent the deterioration of natural resources so that they can continue to furnish the basis for sustained economic development.
2. To anticipate the effects of project implementation which could generate costs that have not been determined following ordinary evaluation procedures.

The guidelines were apparently applied to several projects, including a flood control and irrigation project in Guyana, but that project's appraisal report does not mention the potential environmental impacts.

If the IDB guidelines are implemented, they would improve the Bank's requirements for proper forestation in catchment areas, although there has been little insistence in the case of most dams and irrigation schemes that reforestation or afforestation projects be included. A recent loan of $41.5 million for irrigation in Guerrero, Mexico, was appraised in September 1977. The project documents noted that "certain environmental benefits" could be anticipated, particularly control of damaging floods and certain contaminants to a nearby incipient fishing industry.

Sensitivity to the need to connect reforestation with irrigation projects in the AsDB appears quite impressive. In the case of the Wampu River flood control project (Indonesia), the AsDB made reforestation of seven thousand hectares of catchment area a condition of the loan so as to prevent continuing flooding and siltation. Likewise, the AsDB staff emphasized the need for experts in fisheries management whenever pesticides are used or offshore effects anticipated.

Dams and Irrigation: Concluding Observations

Dam and irrigation projects are considered separately for the purposes of this study, although there are occasions when the two activities are planned simultaneously in a single project.

Least cost solutions for hydroelectric power should fit into overall national energy planning which considers environmental costs and benefits as well as technical and financial characteristics of the various alternatives. Guatemala and Nicaragua have commissioned environmental assessments of their national energy master plans.[11] (These assessments were undertaken *after* the least cost solutions had been selected.) The use of environmental criteria for preliminarily screening all energy alternatives would of course be the optimum approach within the master planning context.

Better still, coordinated regional water use planning could be the key to the environmental improvement of the planning and execution of large water management projects. Because the phased development of hydropower and irrigation in river basins takes many years, involves a plethora of international, national, and regional institutions, as well as a large cast of consultants who may be involved only in discrete portions of the overall development, responsibility is generally diffuse and continuity lacking. This militates against monitoring, research, assessments, and management of problems related to the environmental changes that take place in watersheds, rivers, flood plains, and estuaries.

Guidelines have been introduced to make the planning and execution of water resource projects more environmentally sound, but the guidelines are often incomplete; such major potential problems as spread of disease or secondary effects of pesticides are not always mentioned. Furthermore, the guidelines merely indicate possible effects of development and provide no means to evaluate the costs and benefits associated with the changes. Finally, the guidelines are not always used; with continuing emphasis on single purpose systems, it is likely that they will remain underutilized. Modification and consistent employment of these guidelines are badly needed.

The desirability of beginning surveys and evaluations of environmental aspects of water resource development *prior* to the feasibility study stage is recognized by some institutions. However, at present, no formal linkages exist between the banks and technical assistance agencies, such as the UNDP or the OAS, which conduct prefeasibility studies. Informally, the AsDB sends the World Health Organization (WHO) its monthly operations bulletin which is commented upon, and WHO contacts are listed. The World Bank has not neglected environmental problems in irrigation projects, even taking into account the gap between World Bank and FAO guidelines. Since 1970 it has financed schistosomiasis control measures in twenty projects and succeeded in getting borrowers to undertake control in nine other projects.[1][2]

UNEP could do more to help improve functional coordination of the environmental policies and practices of technical assistance institutions, on the one hand, and financing institutions on the other. For their part, development banks can insist on environmental evaluations in planning and prefeasibility studies prepared by technical assistance agencies (especially the OAS and the UNDP) and thereby use their prestige to encourage the earliest possible consideration of environmental factors. Too often the feasibility study is made too late to effectively include adequate attention to environmental considerations.

Training and planning work in multiple purpose river basin development have been supported by the UNDP, especially in connection with the Committee for Coordination of Investigations of the Lower Mekong Basin, where over $20 million in support has been provided during 1964 through 1976. In addition, a UNDP-funded environmental advisory post was established in 1975 in the Mekong committee to work specifically on this aspect of the basin's development planning.

This type of training and backup in river basin management is worthy of more support. The IIED team recommends that a special task force be set up, possibly by UNEP, to define systematically the needs, scope, and institutional possibilities for evaluating the long-term effects of continuing hydropower and irrigation development on the large rivers of the world.

Water Supply and Waste Disposal

The provision of water for drinking and domestic purposes has traditionally been viewed as an environmentally beneficent activity. The situation was recently well put by the president of a large consulting engineering firm:

In the past, the traditional assumption has been that any unfavorable environmental impact would be insignificant in comparison with the advantages derived from achieving a project's economic or health development objectives. This assumption is now under scrutiny.[13]

Projects are now being questioned because water supply and waste disposal systems are not always considered together, necessary health and nutrition education in conjunction with water supply is not always provided, the systems are often too expensive for the amenity they provide, and there is often no local ability to repair breakdowns.

Those multilateral lending institutions that fund water supply projects have recently given them increasing emphasis. Waste disposal, on the other hand, has been accorded a much lower priority. It appears that these projects are best carried out, or at least planned and designed, in tandem. This section of the chapter focuses on the adequacy of the level of aid lending committed to water supply and sewerage projects and on the treatment of health problems, access, and maintenance.

Both supply and disposal projects are designed to solve an environmental problem: the well-known health risks of impure water. Dysentery is one of the major killers of small children in developing countries; roundworm and hookworm diseases affect a billion people across the globe. Both are spread through lack of sanitary facilities; typhoid and cholera are spread through fecal contamination; and trachoma, an eye disease affecting 500 million people, could be avoided by the simple act of regular washing of hands and face with clean water.[14] This tragic state of affairs is technically soluble, but known solutions have never been widely applied.

In rural areas pesticides are used for crop protection and in both rural and urban areas pesticides are used for malaria control. The health problems associated with the contamination of water supplies by these chemicals must also be considered.

There are a variety of ways to improve water supply in both rural and urban areas—everything from digging shallow wells to providing more sophisticated piping. Two common types of pipe systems are standpipes outside homes and pipe connections within homes themselves. The amount of water used usually increases dramatically with the introduction of house connections, while the problems associated with infested or infected water supplies decrease with the use of both standpipes and house connections, *if* they are appropriately maintained and used by the families provided with them. Water treatment is also used in many circumstances, and the long-term effects of chlorination on human health are now beginning to be understood.[15]

Waste disposal systems also vary tremendously. In some places ground soakaway is relied upon; in others, simple ditches and trenches or more sophisticated drainage and sewer works are employed. An increasing variety of privies are being used with mixed success.[16] Without disposal, many health advances introduced in other projects are lost and new problems arise. Moreover, without adequate user participation and training, water distribution systems often break down and lie unused.

Spending on Water Supply and Waste Disposal

Very often "integrated urban" or "integrated rural" development projects include a component for water supply that is difficult to extract and therefore not included in table 8-1. Based on available documentation, it appears that total lending for water supply and waste disposal has been rising in recent years.

In 1977, World Bank and IDA loans totaled $300.7 million, up from $145.1 million in 1975. An increasing amount of money has been put into mixed (water supply and waste disposal) projects, which have risen from approximately 20 percent of projects in 1971, to an average of over 50 percent in the last two years. Water supply and waste disposal loans are a vital ingredient of a program designed to meet basic needs. Yet this sector still constitutes less than 5 percent of total lending from the World Bank and the IDA. Although this may not seem an obviously inadequate commitment, it is certainly not a sufficient contribution toward reaching the eventual goal of "clean water for all" by 1990 which was endorsed by the U.N. Water Conference in March 1977.

The IDB and the AsDB have long been involved in water supply and waste disposal projects. The IDB is the largest lender for water supply and waste disposal projects in Latin America, as is the AsDB in its region. There has been an increase since 1974 in water supply and waste disposal spending by the IDB, which is a leader in concern for water supply in rural areas. Between 1961 and 1971, for example, IDB loans for rural water supply comprised $65.3 million of the total external borrowing of $68.3 million used in those projects. Indeed, one of the IDB's earliest loans was to improve the water supply of the city of Arequipa in Peru, thus beginning its involvement over a ten-year period to fund water supply projects in the rural areas of Peru. The IDB has attempted to identify an area of need and consolidate lending in it in a given country so as to achieve a significant impact.

The AsDB has funded $322 million in loans for water supply projects in Asia in the period between 1971 and 1976. Water supply and sewerage projects comprised 11 percent of AsDB projects for that period. The total loaned by the Caribbean Development Bank (CDB) through 1976 was $5.7 million with all but two loans going for water supply alone. Water supply and sewerage projects funded by the African Development Bank (ADB) and the African Development Fund (ADF) have been primarily for urban projects, even though 82 percent of the member countries' population is rural. In the 1974-1976 period, the number of these projects increased so that in 1976 it totaled $28.0 Fund Units of

Table 8-1
Water Supply and Sewerage Lending

	No. of Projects	US $ Millions	% of Total Water Supply and Sewerage Loans	% of Total Bank Loans
The World Bank and the Regional Banks[a]				
World Bank 1971-1976				
Water Supply	24	682.1	47.4	
Sewerage	8	141.9	9.9	
Water Supply & Sewerage	29	589.3	41.0	
Other	1[b]	25.0	1.7	
Total	62	1,438.3	100.0	4.4
Inter-American Development Bank 1971-1976				
Water Supply	17	167.6	50.0	
Sewerage	4	46.8	14.0	
Water Supply & Sewerage	10	120.6	36.0	
Total	31	335.0	100.0	5.3
Asian Development Bank 1971-1976				
Water Supply	18	257.6	80	
Sewerage	1	20.0	6	
Water Supply & Sewerage	1	22.0	7	
Other	2[c]	22.7	7	
Total	22	322.3	100.0	11.0
Caribbean Development Bank 1971-1976				
Water Supply	6	5.4	94	
Sewerage	2	.3	6	
Water Supply & Sewerage	0	0.0	0	
Total	8	5.7	100.0	5.1
BADEA 1975-1977				
Water Supply	1	68.0	94.4	
Sewerage	1	4.0	5.6	
Total	2	72.0	100.0	48.8

Other Organizations Studied[d]	US Millions	% of Total Commitment
United Nations Development Programme 1971-1976		
Water Supply & Sewerage	26.5	
European Development Fund 1974-1977 (4th F.E.D.[e]*)*		
Water Supply	27.3	
Sewerage	9.6	
Total	36.9	3.0

[a]ADB figures unavailable.

[b]A solid waste disposal project.

[c]One loan was approved for a desalinization project in Hong Kong in 1972. A second loan, made to Indonesia in 1976, was for urban sanitation.

[d]OAS figures unavailable.

[e]Commitments of the Fourth Fund for Economic Development to December 31, 1977.

Account (FUA) for seven of sixteen projects. The proportion of the ADF share was upwards of 70 percent. The projects have involved water supply (for example, Tanzania for piped water for regional towns, Kilgali, Port Sudan), rainwater drainage (N'Djamena, Chad), and water supply and sewerage (Cape Verde, Senegal). The European Development Fund (EDF) has invested $170 million in the field between 1960-1975: $90 million for urban water supply and $60 million for rural water supply, but only $20 million for sewerage.

The Programs and Procedures of the Banks

Urban Water Supply. The World Bank in its early years emphasized large-scale urban water supply systems, which is still a major focus. The Bank has in a number of instances, such as a project in Bombay, returned to expand facilities in major urban areas, and in other countries (for example, Philippines and Sri Lanka) focused on a number of urban areas in the same project. In some cases, such as Sri Lanka, the Bank's work includes aspects recommended by master plans designed under the sponsorship of UNDP to ascertain the needs of particular urban areas. Unfortunately, by the time the plans are completed growth patterns of the urban area may have shifted.

Sewerage or waste disposal projects are an increasing part of the World Bank's work because the lack of such provisions is increasingly recognized as a significant health problem. A Sri Lankan project emphasized supply, but a separate component provided technical assistance for sewerage design. The sewerage problems in Kingston, Jamaica were serious enough to hold up needed development until new waste disposal facilities were in place. A 1975 World Bank loan providing for waste disposal has enabled this moratorium on building to be removed, permitting construction of desperately needed housing in central Kingston.

Steps have been taken recently at the World Bank to change the pricing structure for water supply to give the poorest greater access to clean water by increasing the charge for services as usage goes up, rather than the other way around. In this pricing system, the first few gallons would be subsidized, and charges would then increase. In the Bombay Municipal Area Project, for example, the proceeds of the charges for services were used to expand the areas which would be serviced by the system.[17]

Unlike the clear organizational focus for managing irrigation and hydroelectric projects, water supply and waste disposal projects at the World Bank suffer from diffused responsibility. The water and wastes advisor in the Central Projects Staff handles all projects concerned with urban water supply and waste disposal, and other projects of a purely water supply, waste disposal nature.

The Urban Projects Division and the Rural Development Division (both of the World Bank) each have a number of projects involving water supply and waste disposal components and are primarily responsible for their drafting and implementation, although the water supply advisor does have an opportunity for review. Although these reviews do offer the opportunity for an evaluation of a project's environmental effects, economic return requirements may make it difficult to carry out environmentally sustainable projects.

The IDB program has put heavy emphasis on water supply and has been less concerned with funding projects for waste disposal. One reason for this is a philosophy of "first things first" that requires that water supply come before waste disposal. A recent IDB urban water supply guide, for example, lists three principal project components: intake, transmission, and distribution. Disposal is not included.[18]

The AsDB has had nineteen urban water supply projects between 1968 and 1977. Of this number, seventeen have been for water supply only; one is for sewerage only; and one is mixed. More recently, the AsDB has attempted to obtain assurances from governments to develop sewerage and waste water components "within a reasonable length of time." When evaluating projects, the AsDB appears to consider environmental factors. The Hyderabad Project (the one mixed project referred to above) requires consideration of water quality, sewerage, drainage, and solid waste disposal in the charge for the feasibility study. In the sewerage project in Hong Kong the government was able to levy a property tax, thus providing the needed local resources.

It was more difficult to ascertain how well some of the factors that are important are considered in the actual implementation of projects. The AsDB has no formal environmental guidelines or sector paper for water supply. There is a "Review of Bank Operations in Water Supply and Sewerage Sector" (1968-1976) which contains no reference to environmental guidelines. A 1977 manual for water supply project appraisal does refer to the health and water quality issues of AsDB projects as part of their social and economic aspects. The checklists called for also include water pollution and health aspects. No indication was obtained as to how this manual has fared in actual use.

Rural Water Supply. Because urban systems can arguably serve more people through a single project and tariff schedules are easier to design, concern with rural water supply came only recently to most banks, despite WHO statistics which showed that in 1970 over 85 percent of the rural population—over one billion people—did not have reasonable access to safe water. In rural areas the health problems are acute, even as it becomes harder to develop a system to supply the dispersed population.

The IDB program is notable for its early concern for rural water supply. Here the goal has been to make the systems self-financing, although it is recognized that this takes several stages. However, water supplied through standpipes is free, while piped supply is metered. Many IDB projects are implemented by the Pan American Health Organization (PAHO), which encourages focus on health and sanitary needs. Latin America has also benefited from hemisphere-wide targets for service, set in the 1960s and in 1972 (Punta del Este and Santiago). This has provided implementing agencies with both goals and a rallying point. In the Dominican Republic and Peru, for example, rural water supply programs were begun and followed up over a long period of years by the IDB in an attempt to meet the goals. Both of these programs innovatively used local institutions and water "promoters" to mobilize the local population in support of the programs and to solve maintenance problems afterwards.

In the early 1970s, the World Bank began to recognize and respond to the overwhelming problems in rural areas. This new emphasis involved a rethinking of the Bank strategies and the development of new technological and economic approaches.[19] As a result, rural water supply is usually part of a broader rural development scheme at the World Bank.

Making the Systems Work

All too often, rural as well as urban water supply and waste disposal systems, once in place, do not work for very long. This can be caused by lack of training, ineffective local institutions, or failure to include the costs of operation and maintenance in the costs of the project itself. Although the World Bank usually includes a training component in its projects to manage, finance, and repair the system, it has been difficult to ascertain whether or not, in fact, training does take place or how effective it is. In a recent project for Zaire the World Bank (through IDA) proposed a several million dollar program to train about 450 staff members over a five-year period to permit effective operations of a new water supply program.

According to some World Bank personnel, the key to the success of a water project is not the technology involved but the effectiveness of the local institutions set up or charged with operating the system. This explains the importance of training, which is paid for by the banks. The quality of personnel varies tremendously, so a virtually identical system may work well in one place while not at all in another.

The World Bank considers the costs of operation and maintenance a local cost. Similarly, the AsDB does not include operation and maintenance costs that it finances. It acknowledges, however, that while there are many systems in place that need repair and that large investments are required for remedial measures, a major problem is the low priority that the entire sector of water supply, and especially the maintenance component, receives. The IDB is unusual and does include operation and maintenance costs of its water projects, since its philosophy is that rehabilitation may well be cheaper than constructing a new system.

At the U.N. Water Conference in Argentina in March 1977, a resolution was passed which urges that "appropriate external assistance should be available in order to assist in building, operating, and maintaining" water supply and disposal systems.[20] If implemented, this would be a welcome change from the usual practice whereby any external role disappears once a water supply system is installed. This recommendation should be supported and followed by the banks. Education and training in how to make the facility work, how to use it, and how to repair it must be an integral part of assuring that a system continues to function. The early and continuous participation of people in the area who will be using the system, and the establishment in the local area of a promoter or advocate of the system to develop choices regarding its location and the type of service offered must also be given greater weight by the lending institutions. External financing is crucial to provide the organizational and institutional backup which enables better operation of systems and maintenance to take place. The work in operation and maintenance must be done by those using the system, but they need help, which they have not to now been receiving.

New Technologies

Many systems have been using unnecessarily complicated technologies which may be too expensive, and certainly have been hard to operate and maintain. One innovative development has been a two-year research project funded through the Water and Waste Advisor in the Energy, Water and Telecommunications Department of the World Bank, which has been trying to identify low-cost or appropriate technology solutions to replace the use of sewers for waste disposal in rural and some smaller urban areas. The project has produced "state of the art" reports on appropriate waste disposal technology and health effects. Instructional materials and field manuals will also be produced. At present, the theories have been developed and the World Bank is evolving a number of pilot projects to apply the results of the research. These projects will attempt to use technologies such as nightsoil collection, biogas plants, composting operations, and forced draft aeration systems for composting nightsoil.

The uses of appropriate technology both for water supply and waste disposal have only recently been considered by the lending institutions. The World Bank program just referred to seeks to use appropriate technologies for waste disposal as well as to join with other groups in the area of water supply. Pilot projects should be found and some of these systems tested to see whether they do in fact provide alternatives to more costly sewers and other large systems.

Each year the World Bank holds a seminar on water supply and waste disposal techniques. Representatives from the other regional banks have sometimes attended these seminars. They are useful not only to learn about new techniques but to exchange a variety of information about project successes and their failures. Regional banks with personnel dealing with water supply problems should consider regular participation in these meetings.

Water Supply and Waste Disposal:
Concluding Observations

To be effective, both urban and rural water supply projects must meet a number of criteria which some of the banks are beginning to understand and adopt.

1. These projects must be part of a broader program of urban and rural development which will provide a range of services for people to improve the quality of their lives.

2. The level or type of service supplied (usually piped water to house connections in the city and a range of options from shallow wells to house connections in rural areas) should be designed to supply service to the maximum number. The system should be adaptable to changing needs.

3. Rural water supply services, in particular, should be designed and installed after full consideration of the cultural needs and dispositions of the populace to be served.

4. Whenever a bank or agency is considering a water supply program, it should either include adequate means for disposing of waste as a component of the project itself, or else indicate that waste disposal will be included at some certain future time. It should at least describe what types of waste disposal appear most appropriate, what the estimated costs will be, and possible sources of funding. The environmental and human health impacts of using waterless alternatives for disposal should also be assessed.

5. Surveys of the number of people who lack an adequate water supply and the kinds of service they require should be financed and, if necessary, organized by the development agencies (in response to a resolution of the United Nations Water Conference). Water supply has traditionally been provided domestically, with only 10 percent of financing provided from external sources. Thus aid agencies should on their own initiative devote increased attention to water supply and waste disposal projects, by helping governments to submit more and better project requests. Without these surveys and encouragement, the role of the aid agencies will continue to be circumscribed by government requests based on inadequate information.

Notes

1. Peter Freeman, *Large Dams and the Environment*, p. 3, (Washington, D.C.: International Institute for Environment and Development, 1977).

2. See table 7-1.

3. According to the annual reports of the World Bank, in 1975 the Bank approved four projects, costing a total of $425 million of which $188 million was provided by the Bank. In 1976 there were again four projects, costing $621 million, of which $188 million was Bank money. In 1977, six projects required a total outlay of $743 million, $209 million coming from the Bank.

4. "Sectoral Policy in the Electric Power Field," Inter-American Development Bank, November 16, 1977.

5. Organization of American States, "Development of a Methodology Model for Integrated Analysis of Environmental Effects Related to the Development of a Hydrographic Basin," Department of Regional Development, Washington, D.C. (1977).

6. The data on amount of land in the world that is irrigated, cultivated, and cultivable are deficient. Estimates by a Scientific Committee on Problems of the Environment (SCOPE) working group of cultivated land range from 1 to 3 billion hectares. The same group estimated that 1 billion hectares could be irrigated although it is not clear whether this is in addition to or includes the 200 million hectares estimated to be under irrigation now (SCOPE, 1976). Revelle estimates that 1.4 billion hectares of the earth's surface are presently cultivated, 160 million hectares are irrigated, and 3.2 billion hectares are arable. Revelle also estimates that 1.1 billion hectares are potentially irrigable. This figure is in "production equivalence" since an irrigated hectare in the tropics that produces three harvests per year is equivalent to three hectares elsewhere that produce only one harvest per year. [Revelle, Roger, "The Resources Available for Agriculture," *Scientific American*, vol. 235, no. 3 (1976):165-178.] According to Revelle, for the whole world, only one-third of the land that is potentially irrigable can be irrigated since the water needs of arable lands in drier climates exceed the flow of rivers in these regions.

7. SCOPE, *Arid Lands Irrigation in Developing Countries*, (1977).

8. A special unit in the Food and Agriculture Organization (FAO), Rome, provides a total of seventy man-years per year of project assistance to the IBRD for preparation of agriculture projects. The Bank pays for 3/4 of the cost of this cooperative program which was begun ten years ago, and which in the 1976/77 period accounted for twenty-seven of the eighty agricultural projects that were prepared for World Bank financing.

9. Through research support, the UNDP is helping find alternatives to pesticides. Three million dollars has been provided to the International Centre for Insect Physiology and Ecology in Nairobi, which emphasizes biological and behavioral control techniques for insect pests.

10. *Guidelines for the Preparation of Agricultural Investment Projects* (Food and Agriculture Organization, Investment Center, August 1977), 28 pp., par. 6.23.

11. R. Tillman and R. Goodland, "National Power Study Prefeasibility Investigation: Environmental Impact Reconnaissance (Millbrook, New York: The Cary Arboretum of the New York Botanical Garden, 1975), and R. Goodland and R. Tillman, "National Energy Master Plan: Environmental Assessment" (Millbrook, New York: The Cary Arboretum of the New York Botanical Garden, 1975). Study prepared for the Instituto Nacional de Electrificacion, Guatemala.

12. See the World Bank's brochure on its schistosomiasis program (1978). This, along with better drainage to correct problems of waterlogging and salinization, was a key aspect of the Egyptian drainage project which was required as a result of effects stemming from irrigating with water from the Aswan Dam. However, the pesticides pollution problem was not dealt with directly in that project, either as a measurable impact or as a problem that required research leading to alternative methods of pest control, although it was dealt with in the Sao Francisco River Basin study.

13. "Environmental Impact of Water Supply Projects in Developing Countries," in *Environment Impacts of International Civil Engineering Projects and Practices* (American Society of Civil Engineers, 1977). Reprinted with permission.

14. For a discussion of health factors, see Robert Saunders and Jeremy Warford, *Village Water Supply* (Baltimore: Johns Hopkins University Press, 1976), pp. 31-52; and Jane Stein, *Water: Life or Death* (Washington, D.C.: International Institute for Environment and Development, 1977), reprinted in *Environment*, May and June-July, 1977.

15. See T. Page et al., "Drinking Water and Cancer Mortality in Louisiana," *Science*, vol. 193 (July 2, 1976):55.

16. For a fuller discussion, see Saunders and Warford, *Village Water Supply*, and "Alternative Approaches to Sanitation Technology," a progress report on World Bank Research Project 671-46, (January 1978).

17. Discussions of rate structures are found in appraisal reports of a number of banks. Some of these questions are raised in Jeremy Warford and P. Rosenfield, "Public Utility Pricing and Pollution Control," in *Environmental Impacts of International Civil Engineering Projects and Practices*, (American Society of Civil Engineers, New York, N.Y., 1977).

18. Terry A. Powers, "Guide for Appraising Urban Potable Water Projects," Inter-American Development Bank, Washington, D.C., (1977).

19. See Sanders and Warford, *Village Water Supply*.

20. United Nations, *Report of the United Nations Water Conference*, E/CONF.70/29 (1977), Resolution II.

Forestry Projects and the Environment

Forests today cover a quarter of the surface of the developing world. They mediate regional climates. They still represent the largest natural habitat resource. But man's competition for their use is growing quickly. The forest is the only fuel source for many of the world's people, the essential raw material for housing and a great range of industries, a priceless resource for recreation, and the habitat and gene pool for an immense variety of natural species.

At present rates of cutting and replanting, the World Bank estimates that within sixty years or about three generations, these forests will disappear completely. Whether, and for what purpose, those forests will be cut down—for timber, pulp, fuelwood, to make space to live, to grow crops, or to graze livestock; whether, and how, they are well managed for sustained yield to meet these needs; whether formerly tree-covered areas that are now abandoned to the ravages of erosion will be rehabilitated for productive use: these are the challenges of forestry development faced by governments and by the multilateral lending and technical assistance communities—indeed by all agencies that offer aid.

In this chapter a wide range of these problems are examined as they affect man's environment. However, it was necessary to exclude discussion of many related environmental impacts. Examples of these are chemical pollution from paper pulp making, the environmental aspects of palm oil production, and the planting of trees for animal feed or for crops such as fruits, rubber, teas, coffee, palm oil, coconuts, or gum arabic.

Remarkably little planting (or even good forest management) has occurred in the developing world, either in an absolute sense, or when compared to the huge areas which have been, and are being, deforested. Responsibility for this state of affairs lies squarely on the governments of the regions, not the international development institutions or other aid giving organizations, for it is the governments in the final analysis who must develop the will and the ability to exploit their forests wisely. Most importantly, they must find alternative sources of fuel or land for poor people who will otherwise destroy fragile environments by cutting trees for fuel, for timber, or for space to cultivate crops and graze livestock because they are living at the margin of subsistence and can see no alternative.

It is essential to stress the limited supporting role to which international development financing institutions are inevitably restricted. They cannot, and should not, impose policies on governments. Nevertheless, aid-giving organiza-

115

tions very often do have a critically important catalytic part to play: they can provide the inspiration and the skills to plan and carry out forestry development; they can provide scarce foreign exchange and in some cases substantial amounts of local currency; perhaps most importantly, they can support such projects with training, institution building, and research.

The principal aim of this chapter, then, is to examine what the multilateral aid institutions are doing in these areas. The concepts and policies of the banks and agencies visited will be reviewed and an attempt made to evaluate the environmental soundness of both these policies and the projects designed to carry them out.

The simple answer to these questions is that most of these organizations are still doing very little. Even the bank most active in forestry projects—the International Bank for Reconstruction and Development (the IBRD or World Bank)—is not yet financing enough imaginative and environmentally sound forestry development. Most of the regional banks have shown little interest in undertaking forestry projects, which they tend to regard as complicated and financially unrewarding. Most of them have no defined forestry policies, nor any foresters on their staff. And most have financed very few forestry projects. Forestry projects are admittedly technically difficult and harder to finance than other desperately needed kinds of development. And it may be that only a few of the institutions reviewed here, perhaps the Inter-American Development Bank (IDB), the Asian Development Bank (AsDB), and the European Development Fund (EDF) should attempt much more in this sector.

Yet, there appear to be new grounds for hope. The World Bank, which probably does the best forestry work of any international aid agency, has adopted an imaginative and environmentally excellent forestry policy. However, even though it has carried out more projects than others, it still has done little in comparison to its accomplishments in other fields.

Forestry Development Policies of the Regional Banks

With the exception of the Inter-American Development Bank (IDB), most of the regional banks still do not have formal forestry policies, and only the IDB and the Asian Development Bank (AsDB) have undertaken *any* forestry development projects.[1]

The AsDB does, however, appear to be taking a growing interest in forestry programs. It is working on a forestry policy paper but still has done little in the way of true forestry development. It has financed a number of palm oil and rubber projects, which are outside this chapter's scope. It has put catchment reforestation requirements in a recent loan to Indonesia for water development, and is reportedly considering a forest development program for northern Thailand, as well as an afforestation and erosion control project in Afghanistan.

In 1977 the AsDB financed two projects: a forestry project in Burma designed to increase the production of teak from Burma's underutilized forests; and the Sagarnath Forestry Development Project in Nepal, designed to replace some eleven thousand hectares of degraded and unproductive forest with fast growing species. The AsDB now has one professional forester and a forest economist on its staff.

Given the recognized fact that forest management and river catchment management constitute the largest environmental problem, and one of the major economic problems, in most of the Asian countries, it is very important for the AsDB to complete and publish a forestry policy paper as soon as possible, and to involve itself more heavily in forest development. Given all the difficulties, financial, technical, and political, inherent in forestry development (for example, throughout Southeast Asia, forestry concessions policy is a sensitive political issue), it is not surprising that so little has been done. The question is how much more should the AsDB attempt to do itself or in conjunction with the World Bank.

In 1977, the IDB issued "Guidelines for the Preparation of Loan Applications for Forestry Development Projects," which provides a good basis for a much more active forestry program than has been carried out to date. The policy paper indicates that the IDB will consider financing all the traditional types of forestry projects. The IDB also offers to undertake the regeneration of natural forests and the establishment of plantations for watershed protection; the planting of forests for the restoration of eroded lands; the establishment of national parks to conserve natural vegetation and wildlife; and planning for the proper use of forest land in colonization schemes. It indicates that it is also willing to give technical assistance, available in some circumstances on a grant basis, for forestry training, research, institution building, market studies, extension services, and carrying out of forest inventory land surveys.

In the face of such a good policy statement on forestry it is remarkable that the IDB has done so little in the way of forestry projects. Moreover, despite its clear recognition of the problems facing Latin America and the need to move ahead, the IDB has not taken enough initiative to urge its members either to undertake forestry development or, with one exception (a tree plantation loan in Uruguay), to build or strengthen new institutions, as its policy papers indicate is essential.

The Forestry Policy of the World Bank

The World Bank extended no forestry loans until 1968, twenty-two years after the founding of the Bank. However, no forestry loan was proposed by a borrower and rejected by the Bank (or suggested by the Bank and not taken up by a borrower) in this earlier period.

In the early 1970s, an important policy change occurred which was to have a profound effect on the World Bank's forestry policy. This was the decision to use its resources increasingly to benefit "the poorest of the poor." In 1972, the World Bank formed a new Agriculture and Rural Development Division to determine how its new concept of concern for the poorest could be turned into appropriate agricultural and general rural development projects. Among the aims of such projects was that of helping poor farmers not to serve as agents of their own undoing by destroying the physical basis of their own livelihood in their search for food and fuel.

Based in part on this experience, in December 1976 the division began to write a forestry development policy paper. It had the participation of every level of the World Bank's management, of most of its divisions, and foresters and other experts outside the Bank, particularly from the Food and Agricultural Organization (FAO) and the United Nations Development Programme (UNDP). This paper, which was completed and approved by the Bank's president in 1977, was skillfully used to focus and evolve the World Bank's thinking on forestry.[2]

Despite some weaknesses, the forestry paper is an excellent, and in fact the only, short statement of the problems and prospects of social and environmental forestry development. Certainly, from an environmental viewpoint it is the best sector policy paper written by *any* development agency. It contains important innovations: it begins with the enunciation of a concept of environmental forestry and calls for substantial resources to be devoted to projects to upgrade degraded forests or restore deforested areas in the ecologically disaster-prone areas—the tropical forests, the steep, well-watered high mountain valleys, and the arid grasslands and savannah threatened with desertification. It assigns high priority to efforts by the World Bank to evolve broadly based national forestry development strategies for developing countries, with special emphasis on rural and environmental forestry issues. Finally, it implies that resources will be found for carrying out well-conceived plans, and promises that in World Bank forestry activities particular emphasis will be given to the environmental and ecological effects of forest destruction. All of this breaks very important new ground.

This forestry sector policy paper has served the additional function of bringing about important changes in the World Bank's forestry lending policy: very importantly, it has achieved Bank agreement to dedicate a substantially larger, if still small, part of its lending capacity to forestry loans. The whole process of coming to an agreement on the forestry policy paper could stand as a model for other areas inside the World Bank, and for other aid-giving organizations.

Traditional Forestry Development at the World Bank

Before examining the World Bank's "new style" forestry development, which will soon constitute the largest number of forestry loan projects,[3] a brief look at the few "traditional" forestry projects financed by the IDB and earlier by the World Bank is necessary. These are defined here as loans for forest planting or management related to a large-scale modern wood-processing industry.

Two such projects are the World Bank's Akdeniz and Balikeser loans to Turkey in 1970 and 1974. Although these loans were basically for paper and pulp mills, the Bank also set out to help the Turkish government reorganize the management of the forest preserves, on which the mills depended for raw materials, to train forest personnel, and to build or improve access roads to these areas. The World Bank also recommended more basic changes in how these degenerated forests could be upgraded and better managed for sustained yield. This also involved helping the Turks to set up more intensive forest protection programs, with special reference to protecting key water catchment areas from overcutting. Although the program included a study of how to improve farm practices and the way of life of people residing in the many surrounding forest villages, the real purpose was to build the paper and pulp mills and to build access roads. Thus, they were not really "new style" loans.

In the last decade only four other industrial afforestation and reforestation projects were approved by the World Bank and one by the IDB. The latter was a rather ambitious project ($17 million just for direct and indirect foreign exchange costs) granted to the Argentine Banco de la Nacion for afforestation and reforestation on a countrywide basis to stop erosion in the mountainous Andean areas and in arid Patagonia; for establishing plantations to replace degraded tropical forests; and for replanting eroded areas cleared for agriculture and cattle raising in the subtropical Missiones area. All of the wood produced is destined for Argentina's wood processing industries, which badly need raw materials. The appraisal documents, very detailed on the financial aspects of the loan, contain little detailed discussion of its environmental aspects.

Apart from the Turkish project, the World Bank's loans for industrial tree plantations have been few and small. In Zambia and Kenya the Bank approved $5.3 million and $2.6 million loans respectively. They were experimental loans for the Bank, although the concept of training local technicians to establish or strengthen local governmental institutions to support them was already established in other types of loans. The 1970 Kenya I loan was particularly interesting because not only was it the first country-wide forestry program, but also it was in many ways the herald of the "social forestry projects" to come. It was designed to establish 100,000 hectares of industrial tree plantation (soil-enriching wattle to provide charcoal for Kenya's cement industry, and pulpwood and saw logs from pine and cypress) and to devise a means of producing this wood under the "taungya" system (an established method for interplanting trees and food crops), hopefully improving the standard of living of some eight thousand families. Despite some difficulties, the project went into its second phase in 1976 with both the Kenyans and the World Bank learning a great deal in the process.

Given the increasing shortage and rising prices of paper and timber in the less-developed countries (LDCs), the World Bank and the IDB should continue to encourage members to apply for loans to expand and improve natural forest management both for timber, paper and pulp production, and for expanding their industrial tree farming programs.

New Style Forestry Development at the World Bank

By now, the World Bank has undertaken a number of new style forestry projects, of which only a few can be examined, or even mentioned. The most interesting, and by most accounts successful, of the World Bank's wood producing programs are the Korean fuelwood project (discussed later in this chapter), and two integrated Philippines forestry projects. The latter two projects were approved in 1974 and 1978 for $2 million and $8 million respectively. The first phase of the Philippines projects involves credit and technical assistance to individual farmers for the planting of 5,000 hectares of fast-growing pulpwood trees to provide much needed raw materials for the Philippine government's integrated paper and pulp operation in Mindanao. What makes it a new style loan is that this project involves, 1,300 poor farmers who had lived in degraded forest and pasture land. The second phase, just approved, calls for the expansion and diversification of the first phase and is to include the planting of about 32,000 hectares of fast growing trees for pulpwood, leaf meal, charcoal, fuelwood, and poles. It involves 7,400 farmers. The project will fulfill a small part of the Philippine government's program for improving land use management in heavily cultivated and overgrazed areas and for strengthening the Philippine forestry service. Although not without problems, thus far the project appears to have survived its nonproductive period. It may also become a model for small farm industrial tree plantations elsewhere in the developing world.

Another type of World Bank project deserves attention: the Bank's recent forestry loans to Nigeria. They constitute a program inevitably fraught with problems, particularly as they involve not only reorganizing and consolidating a number of unsuccessful earlier projects of other institutions, but also establishing forest villages to resettle refugees, particularly in eastern Nigeria where the tropical forests have been devastated by short-sighted use and by war. This loan will involve unusually heavy use of expatriate foresters and administrators.

One interesting departure is a technical assistance credit by the World Bank to India to carry out local species trials. This hopefully will allow it to move ahead with its massive pulpwood and fuelwood programs. The Bank stepped in when UNDP, which normally provides preinvestment assistance, was unable to do so. The World Bank should continue to become more involved in social forestry projects in India.

Projects Where Forestry Development Is Not
the Sole or Major Focus

Rural Development Projects and Agricultural
Development Projects

Although it is clear that many-sided rural development and agricultural development projects constitute the hard core of the World Bank's new style programs,
it is equally clear that forestry development components (and environmental
protection) are further from the center of rural development operations and
thinking than are agriculture and animal husbandry. But that may change with
the approval of the new forestry policy paper, since the World Bank's new
policies provide, rightly, for the integration of a wide range of forestry and
forestry-related components into rural development loans.

For example, in two types of projects (crop and cattle raising) forestry may
play a direct part in promoting the project's central purpose. First, in agriculture
there are schemes for intercropping trees with food and other crops, either as a
permanent system or to provide food or cash crops until the trees are
harvestable. Considerable thought and research has been devoted by the World
Bank to intercropping, which holds particular promise for tropical forest areas.
But as far as can be determined, the only examples incorporated into projects
are in the Kenya forestry projects, where intercropping under the taungya
system is being tried, and in Nigeria, Tanzania, and the Philippines. Future
projects will contain more examples as field research proceeds. Second, in cattle
raising, there are a number of successful examples of planting trees or bushes for
producing leaves for fodder. Experiments in Nepal showed that certain protein-
rich leaves could provide 45 percent by bulk of the food for cattle and 25
percent for buffalo, thus theoretically, at least, reducing very substantially the
demands on badly overgrazed hillside pastures. Examples of World Bank fodder
tree programs are found in a Mauritius rural development project, and a Mali
livestock project, where additional shrubs which could be partially cut during
the dry season were planted. Making this fodder system work will require more
human restraint than technical skill. It probably can succeed only as a product
of a larger system where some kind of protection is provided.

These projects notwithstanding, not all new rural development projects are
examined to see if they should or could contain forestry components. This
should always be done automatically. It is among the best methods at the World
Bank's disposal to enhance environmental protection and to increase environmental awareness of Bank officials and of loan recipients. The Bank's present
forestry staff could not cope with this additional workload and should be
expanded by one position at the very least to make this possible. One final

caveat is well illustrated in a World Bank report on forestry in Nepal. In the report it is stressed that rural forestry programs should be integrated as much as possible with agricultural or rural development projects. According to this line of reasoning, since the local inhabitants, especially those in remote areas, tend to give priority to their perceived short-term needs (roads, water supplies, health clinics, social services and agricultural assistance), then an integrated approach that incorporates long-term afforestation or soil conservation programs must be included as part of an overall development package. By meeting both the perceived short-term needs and the environmentally sound long-term needs, it is more likely that forestry development programs will be successful.

Rural Development Forestry: Fuelwood Programs

Of all the aspects of the world's present energy crisis, none is more destructive to the environment or more painful for the poorest people in the developing world than the rapid disappearance of the trees and brush which provide the great bulk of their fuel supplies.

Every year, women in many of the poorest developing countries have to spend more and more time walking farther and farther to gather wood. In some areas (arid West Africa and Nepal) wood is so scarce that much food which should be cooked is eaten raw. The purchase price of firewood is rising so rapidly that up to 25 percent of income in the Sahel and in some of the Andean regions is now devoted to its purchase. The difficulty is, of course, compounded by the increased cost of fuel oil and kerosene.

Overuse of fuelwood due to excessive population has a domino effect on the environment. Shortage of fuelwood forces people to burn animal dung, and the impact on agricultural productivity of using animal dung and leaves formerly left to enrich the soil for household fuel is catastrophic.

The World Bank (and some of the regional banks) appear to recognize the magnitude of this problem, even though so far only the World Bank and the AsDB have made any fuelwood loans. They also recognize that the failure of past fuelwood projects has very often been the fact that they were imposed on villagers by central governments without consultation or participation of those whom they were supposed to serve and whose lands were often appropriated for the purposes of the project. The World Bank has come to recognize that the populations thus affected must somehow be compensated if their cooperation is to be secured. This is best done in a broader bundle of benefits. Accordingly, the Bank has wisely chosen to approach most of its fuelwood programs through rural development projects.

The World Bank's usual fuelwood approach in rural development projects is to plant fast growing exotic species that have been proved suitable by species trials for local soil conditions. These species often grow as much as twenty times faster than local species. One hectare of this kind of plantation can often provide enough fuel for fifteen to twenty people. Such plantings do not require great technical skill. The problem is to create, within a very few years, large enough woodlots to meet the needs of the villagers of a given area.

Fuelwood projects have proved difficult to carry out for many reasons. These include: the difficulty of building local support, particularly because strong village leadership often must be created; the problem of creating confidence that a fuelwood project will redound to local benefit, either through badly needed fuel or from income from sales to urban purchasers; and the problem of generating local income for workers who depend for their livelihood on fuelwood lots until trees are harvestable. In addition, there are difficulties in securing governments' financial and political support over many years so as to guarantee effective technical assistance to villagers (tools, nurseries, advice on planting, management and cutting, and marketing) until the project is self-sustaining. There is also the problem of finding suitable land: land good enough for planting annual crops, particularly if close to towns, is normally denied to fuelwood projects; on the other hand, land away from villages is much harder to protect.

These difficulties should, however, not be overestimated, as there are successful fuelwood projects sponsored by the World Bank and national governments to serve as models. Experience has taught that the level of technology needed is not as sophisticated as has been thought. Also, average planting costs, often $100 per hectare or less, are lower than had been estimated and certainly quite acceptable.

Surprisingly, in view of the magnitude of the fuelwood crisis, very little has been done by the multilateral development banks. The regional banks have done no fuelwood projects, and the World Bank has so far financed only eight, although it has a further twelve in preparation. Early Bank projects were small, and not particularly successful because of lack of public support and high associated costs such as terrace and road building; others suffered because the plantations were so far from villages.

More recently, in Colombia, the World Bank financed a large fuelwood program which was part of a multifaceted agricultural program. Another interesting project was in Senegal. Its fuelwood component was designed as part of a groundnut planting rural development scheme and had important environmental protection elements. Eucalyptus and acacia trees were planted in strips to combat erosion; they also are being cut for fuel and poles, a technically difficult concept, but worth trying.

By far the most successful and largest bank-financed fuelwood project to date is the $3 million Korean program approved in 1976 by the World Bank as part of a large, all-purpose agricultural project. The fuelwood part of the project, already established before the World Bank approved its loan, calls for the planting of 50,000 hectares of trees (70 percent for fuelwood, 30 percent for timber) on largely denuded Korean hills, which are too steep for agriculture. Trees are also planted in strips along roads and streams, and bush clover, which can provide a substantial amount of fuel in one year, is planted between fields. Even private land is compulsorily planted by village forestry associations, with the private owners receiving 10 percent of the wood. Despite problems with logistics, supervision, and technical support, the project has already begun to transform the Korean fuel situation.

Fuelwood represents an area ripe for greatly increased development activity of a kind that could be highly beneficial to the environment. Technical data good enough to sustain a major campaign are at hand (on species, planting, maintenance, and cutting, and for every major region). There is also enough experience accumulated about the serious problems of gaining local support and participation in fuelwood projects to justify such an initiative. Much of this experience comes from outside the international development community, as most fuelwood projects (many of them disasters with important negative lessons) were launched by less-developed country governments, or their colonial predecessors.

Technical and human problems differ considerably from project to project, and it takes time to find the right technical solution, to build local confidence and support, and to ensure long-term central government backing. The way ahead is to start on a small but significant scale in as many regions of as many needy countries as possible. It is true that in some areas additional practical research is desirable on new fast-growing species, on the use of marginal lands in various ecological zones, and on more efficient wood combustion. But the principal need is to get started now, to move ahead as soon as possible with plantations large enough to meet regional fuel requirements. Fuelwood requires high-priority attention.

Who is going to assume worldwide leadership for such a campaign? Leadership by any one country or group of countries would not be acceptable. Leadership by the United Nations or any one of its Specialised Agencies might be too weak and too politicized. The World Bank should consider accepting responsibility for organizing this effort. A model could be found in other consortia of countries and international aid-giving organizations organized by the World Bank. The problem is to create a strong catalyzing force by focusing a new level of attention and concern.

One must not underestimate the difficulties which would be faced by such a consortium. There is little reason to believe that the governments concerned, even with all the help they could get from the consortia, will plant the millions of trees needed in time to forestall much greater suffering in many parts of the world. But the risks of not acting are so great that even a partial solution is very well worth the effort.

Rural Development Forestry: Land Protection Components

In the spectrum of rural development projects there is a welcome and growing number of forestry components devoted to the protection of trees or forests per se, or to the protection of land by trees; the latter is central because the success of many projects—cropping or cattle raising activities—depends on the continuing good condition of the soil on which that project is being carried out. These are environmental projects in the strict sense. The protection may be indirect. For example, in arid areas of Africa, cattlemen have long overcut and destroyed the wild fodder trees on which their animals browse and depend for food in the driest season. Here the World Bank is trying to protect the local environment with rotational grazing schemes which will in turn reduce the impact on trees and pasture.

Loans to control and correct soil erosion directly constitute another broad category of projects. These are still not widely supported, in part because of their very tenuous economic justification. Projects undertaken include sand dune or sandy soil stabilization in Niger and Senegal, and later in Mali and Upper Volta; catchment area reforestation or management in Colombia, Nepal, Kenya, Pakistan, and Turkey; and establishment of forest reserves on steep and easily eroded slopes in Colombia and Nepal. In this last example, a number of small subprojects were designed to protect roads and irrigation works from erosion and destruction. This is to be done by building small check dams, by replanting trees, by otherwise stabilizing slopes which threaten to slide, and in a somewhat different context, by designing forestry units to aid in flood control, as in the Evros Rural Development Project in Greece. The World Bank has done well to push in this direction, but should do much more.

Development Projects That Could Destroy
Forests: Siting Problems

Some nonforest projects involving potential forest destruction are environmentally inappropriate: clearing forests for urban construction or other human settlements; for agriculture or cattle raising; or for roads or railroads. The banks are correct in agreeing that forest land be cleared when it can be transformed for higher paying productive uses. But in this setting certain difficult choices must not be avoided: some forests should be kept near cities and in the countryside for erosion control, for fuelwood, for protection of endangered species, or for preserving a better human environment. Theoretically, these factors are taken fully into consideration by all the banks. But in practice the banks too often have not taken a strong enough stand against forest clearing. All such projects should be reviewed at a very early stage to ensure that project terms of reference mandate appropriate environmental analysis.

The World Bank and the IDB have become increasingly involved in colonization projects. In the great majority of cases, the space for new agricultural settlements can be found only by cutting down tropical forests. This issue is described in detail in chapter 6. Here it only remains to reiterate that the tropical forests are disappearing so quickly that some kind of early action is needed to stop this destruction. To get effective national action in this regard will require an international conscience-raising effort of major proportions, in which the multilateral development institutions can play a role but probably not provide the leadership. At present, their most important contribution would be to remain involved in the planning and execution of colonization projects, to guarantee at least some degree of environmental soundness.

**Building a Framework for Environmentally Sound
Forestry Development: The Role of the Banks
in a Dialogue with Developing Countries**

Institution building is a third innovative aspect of new style forestry development. In developing countries, sustainable forestry development is too often not possible until new institutions are created or old ones overhauled. Except very occasionally, as noted, the regional banks have done little in this regard.

Even though the banks recognize both the opportunity and the responsibility of their position, they should be ready to take greater initiative in starting dialogues with the governments concerned. Dialogues so begun can continue over years and even decades if constructive on both sides.

The best evidence seems to indicate that the IDB has not yet approached Latin American governments with the aim of stimulating forestry development. This year, however, the IDB may, for the first time, propose some forestry projects to Argentina, Brazil, Colombia, and El Salvador in connection with visits of the Bank's annual country missions. Nevertheless, because of the narrow range of its forestry activities and its great sensitivity to sovereignty issues, the IDB is more likely to respond to country initiatives than to make any of its own.

In contrast, the World Bank has initiated dialogues with a small but growing number of governments, with the ambitious objective of bringing about the development of broadly based forest development policies and strategies in each major forest country. In the World Bank's view, such comprehensive planning can emerge in most developing countries over time, even from often modest beginnings.

Laws and Regulations

The World Bank attaches great importance to helping developing nations prepare and revise forestry laws and regulations. It is prepared to finance this kind of assistance, usually through the IBRD/FAO Cooperative Program or consultants.

Several of the banks believe that to attract investors, timber producing countries must have clear laws on forestry concessions and incentives including practical and enforceable reforestation. The World Bank goes further in two particular aspects: first, it urges the establishment of strong mechanisms and incentives for forest protection. (The Malaysian law framed with World Bank assistance is a good example.) Second, it is Bank policy to encourage and assist developing countries to process its own timber exports locally, rather than to export logs. The environmental aspects of timber processing, although of great environmental significance, fall beyond the scope of this chapter.

Building and Strengthening Forestry Institutions

Forestry institutions must be strengthened because their combined deficiencies presently constitute the principal block to better forestry development in most developing countries. Forest services are weak; up-to-date technical know-how, particularly of planning techniques, is lacking; funding for forestry activities is in short supply; and forest protection activities are politically vulnerable.

In practice, forest institution formation and strengthening means, first of all, financing and arranging the training of forest service personnel, both lower level forestry technicians as well as higher and middle level officials and planners. It also means giving continuing advice on this broad subject. It means, too, helping those institutions plan and execute their plans, bolstering the status of the forest service with other agencies, particularly the finance ministry. Much of this is done through experts financed and recruited through the IBRD/FAO Cooperative Program. Its impact on environmentally sound forest development and protection may, in practice, prove critical.

The IDB has been involved in institution building only in Uruguay, which applied for a tree plantation loan and was told it must establish—and would be assisted in establishing—a competent forest service before a loan would be granted. Institutional weakness in forestry is particularly grave in Latin America, which, although it has one-fourth of the world's forest resources, has undoubtedly the weakest concepts of forestry and the weakest institutions for forest management of any of the developing regions. It is obvious that these problems, and the even more serious problem of progressive deterioration of Latin America's tropical forests and rapidly eroding mountains, must be addressed quickly and systematically, and the IDB should undertake at least a part of this urgent task.

Training

The World Bank (IBRD) through its Cooperative Program with the Food and Agriculture Organization (FAO) will finance forestry training whenever asked by borrowers. At present it is financing some form of training for forestry personnel in every country in which it has forestry programs. Most forestry training, particularly on the higher scientific and planning levels, is still given outside the country or regions at universities or research institutions. However, both the World Bank and the IDB would prefer to offer as much training as possible, particularly at the lower levels, in the country concerned.

The World Bank is also willing to help create, finance, and support new forest training institutions. Only two loans, to Liberia and the Congo, have been given specifically for creating a forest service school, although a program is planned for Nepal. Through the FAO Cooperative Program, the World Bank has contributed to the creation or strengthening of forestry training institutions in a whole range of countries. Bank-supported forestry training institutions are potentially one of the best ways to multiply the spread of knowledge about environmental forestry, and the World Bank should pay special attention to using this potential.

Planning

The desire of the World Bank to establish a capacity for overall land planning in developing countries, and to obtain an understanding of land value planning as a tool in forestry, is potentially of great environmental benefit. Results have not yet been outstanding because of a lack of political will on the part of governments to make the hard choices involved. Despite these difficulties, major efforts should be continued by the World Bank and by the UNDP to encourage the creation of a real forestry planning capacity in all the principal forest countries eligible for World Bank loans. Integrated planning for tropical forest exploitation is of particular importance.

In establishing planning capacities, work on forest inventories is of capital importance. The information generated must be produced in a form useful not only to forest planners but also to government officials and businessmen who too often must decide how much to offer and how much to charge for timber concessions without a realistic idea of what volume, kind, and quality of timber are available. The World Bank has financed forest inventories in a few countries directly, and the UNDP through the FAO has financed a number of others. With World Bank and UNDP/FAO help, developing countries with major forestry interests are now gradually creating their own capacity to do land planning and carry out forest inventories. If done correctly, such planning and inventorying (that is, within the right terms of reference) inevitably heighten environmental awareness.

Research

The IDB, as a matter of policy, finances Latin American national agricultural research institutions, but so far no forestry institutions, or even programs, have been involved. The World Bank, on the other hand, tries to include some research component in each one of its forestry development programs, as it does with many other categories of development. Most of this is research connected to a particular project: species trials; adaptation trials; burning experiments; cutting combinations, and so forth.

Generally this research is carried out by developing country scientists or technicians, with help, encouragement, and financing from World Bank staff members and consultants. Although the data developed by this research is generally project-oriented, it often has practical value. However, routine ways should be found to evaluate Bank-generated research from a broader viewpoint and disseminate it to others in developing countries facing similar problems.

Broader and more theoretical research is also supported by the World Bank and the IDB. This work is carried out by a number of organizations, including such groups as the institutes set up by the *International Consultative Group on Agriculture,* the so-called Bellagio Group. This group, which includes as cofinancers a number of national aid-giving organizations, has supported a whole range of institutes, including particularly the International Institute of Tropical Agriculture (IITA) and the International Crop Research Institute for Semi-Arid Tropics (ICRISAT). So far, however, none of these very important institutes has undertaken the kind of broader research on environmentally oriented forestry and forestry-related problems which appears to be so badly needed: development of low cost catchment afforestation and soil conservation techniques; economic research into quantifying the environmental benefits of forestry development; cheaper land use planning systems; agro-forestry crop combinations (now being undertaken by the promising International Council for Research in Agro-Forestry); and research into low cost, efficient wood burning and heating techniques. One or two of the present institutes (probably ICRISAT and IITA) should agree to undertake some research on these urgent problems.

Roadblocks in the Path to Better Forestry Development

If some of the changes proposed or recommended here are to be carried out, the banks must ask themselves whether they are devoting sufficient manpower and money to forestry development. The clear answer is that they are not. Until quite recently forestry was accorded a very low priority by all the development banks. Some reasons for this, and the major difficulties that still impede greater devotion to environmentally sound forestry projects, can be singled out.

1. Forestry loans, especially those with social or environmental objectives, have been economically questionable: the direct commercial benefits—wood and wood products—cannot be realized because of the slow maturation of most standing timber, while the social and environmental benefits tend to redound to a country or a whole region rather than principally to the growers of the trees. Moreover, the indirect benefits—to soils, to rivers, to downstream inhabitants of river basins—tend to be long-term. These costs are considered hard to quantify,

although progress is being made on this score. Finally, the risks attached to forest investment and the opportunity costs are high, and little long-range employment is generated.

2. The amount of foreign exchange needed for forestry plantation loans is small. Since the banks have very limited ability to cover local currency costs, this makes for small loans with high administrative costs of the kind that banks try to avoid.

3. Governments of developing countries seeking outside assistance for development are not attracted to forestry loans because of the low foreign exchange component and because the lender's local currency contributions are so small, leaving most of the financial and substantial administrative load in their hands.

4. Banks prefer loans with early and visible results, and ones that provide leverage with borrowers on the other difficult matters. These advantages rarely accrue to forestry loans.

5. Forestry management and forestry development often impinge on governments' policies regarding forestry concessions. This raises highly sensitive political questions, since very often these concessions are a prime source of funds for governments in power.

6. Areas of sufficient size available for forestry development tend to be land not good enough for agriculture, which are isolated geographically from activities in the modern economic sector. Forestry projects often require the construction of expensive access roads, which open areas to "spontaneous" colonization with all its consequences.

7. Many forestry projects can only be successful if there is unusually good discipline among, or control over, people from surrounding areas. This is very difficult to achieve.

8. In the end, the greatest difficulty is the impact of rapidly growing populations in the developing world.

All of this encourages a cautious view of forestry lending by the international institutions. How fast could development banks realistically expand their forestry lending?

In many cases, the first essential is to get started. In the case of the regional banks, each should consider making *some* beginning. However, in view of the current weakness of their forestry expertise and their lack of environmental assessment capacity they might start by undertaking joint projects. This is particularly important for the African Development Bank (ADB) because of the importance and potential of forestry development on that continent. The ADB should probably recruit a forester. In the case of the IDB, joint projects would also be beneficial and they too should recruit an environmentally oriented forester. As for selected allocation of funding for forestry, the regional banks should consider starting by putting aside around 1 percent of their budgets for forestry development, and should in their project identification missions urge governments to undertake forestry development projects, particularly those involving soil erosion control and other environmental protection.

The more difficult question is the forestry staff and budget of the World Bank. Stepped-up activity should be undertaken in the following areas: fuelwood activities; more forestry components in a larger number of rural and agricultural projects; a beginning on tree-planting soil conservation projects unconnected with other projects; more intensive involvement in encouraging and financing forestry development research; and more activity in creating a forest planning capacity in developing country governments. A great deal of this is already anticipated in the World Bank's forestry sector paper, which calls for a quintupling of the Bank's budget for forestry over the next five years to a lending target of $100 million annually, a budget level which has apparently been approved by the Bank's top management. This seems to be a level adequate to accomplish the suggested tasks, although it should be examined yearly for possible upward revision.

The World Bank also plans to expand the number of staff foresters from its present six (two in the Agriculture and Rural Development Division, two in the African Division, one in the Latin American Division, and a new forester in the Office of Environmental and Health Affairs) to roughly ten in two years. This expansion should be adequate for the Bank's new proposed level of forestry commitment, bearing in mind the desirability of also adding a soil specialist with forestry experience.

Planning for the Future

It seems possible, in planning for future forestry development, to discern the direction in which environmentally oriented forestry development should evolve and how this might affect the agencies reviewed. Support and demand for assistance in forestry development is likely to increase in the less developed countries, particularly as people in those countries become more concerned about the fuelwood problem, as they try to reduce their dependence on the industrial powers for timber and particularly paper, and as their present concern about erosion and environmental degradation grows.

It is almost a truism to say that forestry development will have to undergo some important changes in the next decade to meet these new challenges. One common theme will be concern for more effective environmental protection. Three coming trends may be discerned which will require aid-giving agencies to rethink their forestry development concepts:

1. *New concepts of international responsibility for conservation.* In place of a degree of suspicion on the part of poor countries regarding the interest of industrial countries and international organizations in conserving poor regions' resources (including their forests), we anticipate demands for international help

in resource conservation. From this is likely to come a better defined and refocused concept of forestry for environmental protection, just as traditional forestry has already evolved towards social forestry. This could result in quite new project formulations.

2. *New leadership roles* for the multilateral development financing institutions in developmental forestry. The problems faced by developmental forestry in producing fuelwood and the disappearance of the tropical forests will require strong, technically competent international leadership such as the highly politicized United Nations and its Specialised Agencies will find hard to supply. In many ways the World Bank is an ideal organization to provide quiet leadership of this kind, above all because of its reputation for technical competence.

3. *New types of financing.* We foresee a requirement for new types of concessional financing from development banks, for environmental protection and even for the rehabilitation of degenerated natural areas which go beyond present definitions of forestry. Such financing could stimulate projects which otherwise would not be started by most developing countries. In particular, there is a need to find ways for development banks to contribute more towards the local currency costs of forestry projects which enhance forest resources.

To sum up, forestry development is a growth industry in which imagination and flexibility on the part of international development banks and the other members of the international community will pay major social and environmental (and in the longer run, major economic) dividends, particularly for the poor.

Notes

1. AsDB's few forestry projects are discussed here for simplicity's sake. It was not possible to evaluate adequately the forestry projects of the European Development Fund without field investigations, which were beyond the range of this study.

2. The World Bank has issued the paper as a Sector Policy Paper, "Forestry," in March 1978.

3. These are projects connected with rural development and aimed at providing jobs—or wood—for the rural poor.

10 Conclusions and Recommendations

Individual chapters of this book contain conclusions and, in some cases, recommendations that relate to particular institutions and sectors. Those are not repeated here. Rather, this chapter treats some of the more general questions that were identified in both the earlier and later phases of the study.

Conclusions

It is undoubtedly a measure of the impact of worldwide public concern, not only over some dim global limits, but at the immense impact of today's developmental capacities, that awareness of resource scarcities and threats to natural systems has penetrated the consciousness of most individuals interviewed during this study. Some of these individuals do not consider environmental problems to be a high priority, and thus the view of environment as simply an additive factor, either to be avoided as an inessential luxury or to be tacked on to the traditional development project, can still be found in every one of the institutions visited.

A wide gap remains between the increasingly alert concern of individuals and the official response of most institutions. Chapters 2 and 3 showed how the World Bank and the Inter-American Development Bank (IDB) have developed a greater environmental awareness and sophistication than other development organizations studied.[1] The Organization of American States (OAS) has, in specific sectors, also demonstrated a keen awareness of environmental problems in its work. The U.N. Development Programme (UNDP), though headquartered in New York, and the European Development Fund (EDF), headquartered in Brussels, experience a far greater diffusion of government control, while their decentralized organization appears to have diffused the influence of donor country environmental concern. The other institutions studied, which are headquartered in developing countries, appear to be equally or more remote from developed countries' environmental consciousness, even though developed countries are in most cases represented on their boards.

This study was undertaken at a time of sharp intellectual transition within the nine institutions surveyed. The uncertainty that characterizes the approach of most multilateral aid institutions to environmental priorities reflects a much larger redefinition of purpose which presently engages them. The troublesome dichotomy of being simultaneously financial and developmental institutions, also concerned with helping to provide basic human needs, has only recently been articulated within them. Taking "environment" into account as one of many considerations before making a loan can be a difficult and slow process, precisely because among all the factors newly being considered, its effects are often most removed in time from the loan and therefore most unlikely to be accounted for by traditional financial methodology.

The need for concessional development assistance is so great in every developing country that the banks approach any innovation that might slow or inhibit the flow of aid with great caution. Only the World Bank has relevant experience with the establishment of environmental standards and review procedures, which have not been found to delay projects. But the suspicion exists in most banks that delays would be an inevitable result of greater environmental concern.

These constraints reinforce a more troublesome barrier to change. Many of the recommendations made in this book could only be implemented if funds were increased for a particular sector or subsector. This can be accomplished in two ways—through the reallocation of available funds or the acquisition of additional funds. The multilateral aid agencies visited argue that it is difficult to reallocate funds or personnel among sectors, because there will always be an important, legitimate constituency whose interests, consequently, are threatened. Thus, it is far easier to add new priorities than to realign existing ones. In practical effect, this means that environmentally sustainable projects can generally be emphasized only as the soft funds available to an organization are increased, which itself has sometimes been difficult to achieve.[2]

Moreover, fears that environmental criteria will add to the cost of traditional "modernization" projects have by no means vanished. (See chapter 2.) The World Bank has claimed that environmental considerations have added no more than 2-3 percent of such projects' costs, but this experience has not been adequately documented and publicized and is not sufficiently familiar to other development financing institutions studied.

A commitment to sustainable development raises a new sort of political issue for development agencies. A recipient government may recognize that its long-term interests will best be served by an environmentally sustainable project, but it may nevertheless believe that its immediate needs compel it to choose short-term advantages. In practice, this inherent conflict seems to exist in fewer instances than might be imagined, as modifications at initial stages to the plan or design of a project very often can offer the same shorter-term yields or results with lower long-term risks of damage. Nevertheless, suspicion of long-term issues was commonly found among planners and decision makers in each development institution visited.

Naturally the attitude of aid-receiving governments towards the environmental activities of development banks occupies a position of paramount importance. The 1977 Development Assistance Committee (DAC) Review's general comment on aid programs applies equally well to the environmental policies and procedures of the banks:

> Donors have an obligation to make their views known to governments on priorities in development policy as they see them. However, attempts to force their views will only breed resentment and failure and could very well lead to increased confrontation which would only make it even more difficult to arrive at the concerted action needed to fight world poverty. What dialogue and advice, mixed with compassion, cannot achieve will not be achieved.[3]

Generalization about the receptiveness of borrower governments towards environmentally improved lending is obviously impossible. One can, however, point to an apparent lack of close liaison between the multilateral development financing community and the departments or agencies of recipient governments charged with environmental planning responsibility. There are notable exceptions to this defect, especially in the case of the role of certain UNDP Resident Representatives who manage in some cases a valuable degree of coordination between the U.N. Environment Programme (UNEP) and national officials with environmental responsibilities in evolving country programs for technical cooperation. Finally, in a few cases governmental receptivity has clearly outstripped the capacity of the banks to provide the detailed, sophisticated environmental advice and expertise that is desired.

In addition to these general observations, the study identified four more specific environmental deficiencies among development financing institutions. The first has been amply illustrated in the body of the report: most of the institutions visited lack any clear procedures for the environmental assessment of their projects. This seems to be true even where environmental awareness has informally surfaced among concerned staff. Notable exceptions are the World Bank and the OAS, although the situation is changing quite quickly, and they may soon be joined by others.

Given a generally still primitive approach to the subject, the second deficiency—a general lack of criteria for assessing environmental impact—is hardly surprising. Again, this was evident in visits to all but one of the banks involved in the study, as is reflected in the foregoing pages. The absence of criteria stems in large measure from the lack of conceptual definition as to what should be considered as belonging to environmental concern. The question of suggesting appropriate criteria for assessing environmental impacts falls beyond the scope of this study, although at various points current requirements as expressed in sectoral manuals and policy papers have been singled out for urgent attention. For example, some of the recent progress by the World Bank in the forestry area deserves attention and perhaps emulation by other institutions.

A third clear deficiency is that no organization has yet succeeded in using alternative forms of analysis and accountancy which include long-term social and environmental effects of development projects.[4] Examination of specific projects in the four sectoral areas confirms this general impression. It is clear that, on the theoretical side of environmental assessment, there is no more urgent task than that of developing and introducing credible means of assessing longer term costs and benefits

In fact considerable progress has been made in this endeavor in some quarters, though knowledge of it has not reached most of the institutions studied. There is a growing literature on "environmental economics," mainly concerned with extending the established framework of welfare economics and cost/benefit analysis to deal with environmental matters. For the most part this is done in a theoretical way. Principles for environmental evaluation are now quite generally established and are becoming more widely accepted. What has not yet, however, been widely attempted is to apply them in practice to project preparation on a ystematic basis. Practical solutions are available and have been used in particular cases, but people concerned with project evaluation in planning offices or development banks are still left without much useful general guidance.[5]

At least two of the institutions reviewed have begun to grapple with the quantification of social costs and effects. At the World Bank there has been a great deal of discussion of these issues in education and other social projects.[6] A panel convened by the World Bank has reported on its attempt to quantify the health benefits of water supply,[7] and the project methodology unit in the IDB has carried on its own set of inquiries. At a more general level, UNEP has commissioned a study at Sussex University, United Kingdom, which identified many of the methodological problems that arise and made a number of useful suggestions.[8]

It was not possible to survey in detail the work being done in the banks and elsewhere on these questions. However, a short discussion of methodologies for environmental impact appraisal, with recommendations, may be found in appendix B.

The fourth specific conclusion concerns the lack of personnel with training appropriate to the task of ensuring proper consideration of the environmental dimensions of development projects. Throughout this book, instances have been noted where the activities of one or two dynamic individuals with ecological or resource management training in a substantive division of an agency have (as in the case, for example, of forestry at the World Bank) transformed a situation. But these exceptions only serve to demonstrate the wide application of the rule.

Recommendations

Each of the studied institutions varies from the others in so many ways, that these suggestions must necessarily remain rather general. They were formulated bearing in mind the limited, supporting role necessarily taken by a development agency in its cooperation with governments.

1. *The multilateral development banks and technical assistance agencies surveyed should publicly commit themselves, at the highest level, to environmental protection and environmental improvement, and should periodically reiterate their policy.* The agencies' commitment should be expressed in official statements of governing bodies and top administrators, and in public documents and annual reports. The leadership of these organizations should stress the message that environmentally sound development must by definition be development that is sustainable over the long run. They should, where possible, take the lead in drawing governments' attention to deficiencies or possibilities in their development planning and project preparation.

2. *These banks and agencies should, where they have not already done so, establish practical procedures for evaluating the environmental soundness of their projects and programs.* Although the scope and details of these arrangements must be decided upon by each organization, there are certain concerns which should be considered in each case:

a. *Procedures for the application of environmental principles should embrace every phase of the project cycle, but in particular should apply to the early stages of project identification, and should extend beyond the formal approval of a project, into its construction, operation, and evaluation.* Supervision and review should not be limited to financial aspects of a project, and projects should be subjected to a final review as a matter of course to see if all objectives were reached.

b. *The environmental procedures adopted should provide positive guidance to agency officials, on the basis of which their planning can be done and against which their performance can be measured.* Guidelines as they have been used to date can be useful, but in many cases they are nothing more than checklists (see chapter 8). A checklist may provide only negative guidance in that it lists problems but does not ordinarily convey the subtlety and complexity of solutions. More importantly, the publication of guidelines has too often been taken as an end in itself, rather than as a means toward better project planning. Thus, it is important not just to prepare guidelines, but to provide guidance. In some cases standards and criteria can be used. In others, general environmental discussion can be incorporated in sector papers and other policy documents.

c. *Country and sector missions should include an environmental dimension.* An increasing number of institutions carry out these missions, which help countries to identify and prepare project proposals. These missions should reflect the environmental priorities established by each institution, which would assist governments in submitting environmentally sound project proposals. Written reports should discuss environmental problems encountered and solutions recommended.

3. *The banks and agencies surveyed should assign responsibility for monitor-*

ing environmental performance and for increasing environmental awareness to specific individuals within the organization. This report does not recommend specific organizational arrangements that can best improve environmental analysis in a specific bank. Each of the nine bodies studied has unique characteristics and a general solution does not exist which will serve all. To suggest a specific environmental office might therefore be best for some groups, but not for others. But in every case, there is a need for a person or persons to have responsibility for the adoption of environmental procedures and practices, and for enhancing the understanding of sustainable development within the institutions. Finally, efforts to raise environmental awareness among the staff at large must not be considered of secondary importance, because the application of procedures cannot be effective unless operational staff accept their importance and are committed to their implementation.

4. *The lessons learned from both environmental successes and failures should be collected and communicated to the staff.* Responsibility for synthesizing material from completed projects, and use of this material for consciousness-raising and developing more appropriate standards, is a critical function. It should be carried out systematically and incorporated into existing staff training programs.

5. *The regional banks, the World Bank, the UNDP, and the OAS should arrange better mechanisms for mutual cooperation in developing and implementing their environmental strategies and policies.* Regional banks often have substantial experience with the environmental problems and opportunities of their regions, which should prove extremely useful to the World Bank, as well as to the UNDP. The regional banks, on the other hand, ought to draw upon the considerable experience accumulated by the World Bank in this area. Such cooperation must not, however, be permitted to impinge on the independence of the regional banks.

6. *The banks and agencies should establish or strengthen their ability to respond favorably to requests for assistance, for strengthening national and local institutions, for training programs, and for help in formulating environmental legislation.* [9] These activities are particularly important because the receptiveness of the intended beneficiaries ultimately determines the value of any development policy.

7. *Far closer cooperation is needed between the banks studied and recipient governments who are, or should be, responsible for setting environmental guidelines for various types of economic development projects.* An example of a useful initiative in this area is the program of case studies of national environmental assessment that has been conducted from UNEP's regional office in Bangkok. Its progress and findings should be communicated to the management of the AsDB and other interested development banks and financing institutions of the region. Latin America would seem a particularly fruitful field for a parallel exercise: particularly so because, as is clear from findings in earlier

sections, the World Bank and IDB are now gearing up for a major expansion of environmentally related projects on this continent.

8. *Within and without lending institutions, efforts to revise project appraisal methodologies deserve greater support.* Promising approaches to new tools for environmental analysis are being undertaken in a number of quarters. Existing literature may or may not prove helpful in actual use, but the need now is to get such analysis sufficiently refined and practically adaptable for it to become an integral part of project preparation work in all institutions.

9. *Recruiting and training of staff must be reconsidered if environmental procedures are to be effective.* First, training of all staff should incorporate an exposure to environmental aspects of development. Second, it is certainly necessary to use ecological and environmental consultants on a regular basis, and it would be useful in environmentally sensitive sectors to have more full-time staff members with environmental training. Banks with regular training courses should consider instituting a special course on environmental aspects of development planning and should seek to include staff from other development institutions and governments in such courses.

10. *Development institutions must devote more time and effort to consulting the persons actually affected by environmentally sensitive projects.* Such projects frequently depend for their success upon detailed knowledge of and special adaptation to local populations' requirements and condition. Too often, the affected population has not been consulted in the planning and execution of projects, for example in agricultural, forestry, and colonization projects, with the result that avoidable mistakes are needlessly committed. It is particularly important to have such consultations in areas of overpopulation, where land and other resources are in diminishing supply. Likewise, services such as water supply and waste disposal or shelter assistance, have often been designed to standards and costs that the user population, if consulted, might not have wanted.

11. *The multilateral development banks should take the lead in encouraging and supporting a new type of project to foster environmental restoration.* Very few resources have so far been devoted to such projects as soil conservation and restoration; deforestation and afforestation for soil protection and fuelwood; and restoration of wetlands and fisheries. For a combination of human and technical reasons, such projects are hard to carry out and therefore tend to be resisted by development institutions. However, increasingly, practical interest has appeared in developing countries, and urgency is lent by a growing recognition of the disappearance of the world's tropical forests, the galloping desertification of formerly productive grasslands, and the catastrophic erosion of mountain regions causing effective destruction of downstream development. The international development banks are well positioned to encourage an effective national and international response to these interrelated crises, and should do so.

It is highly unlikely that any one institution will immediately adopt all of these recommendations as a means of incorporating an environmental dimension in its work. Indeed, the ideal of sustainable development will undoubtedly be best served in any given institution by a commitment to open-mindedness and flexibility, coupled in many cases with an urgent reconsideration of policies and procedures. The authors do not presume to have put forward conclusive answers to any of the important issues raised in the debate on environment and its relationship to development. However, it is certainly to be hoped that publication of this external, comparative survey is not the end of an inquiry, but one small stimulus toward the continuing evolution of a larger, badly needed process within the institutions themselves. The search for practical solutions is, and must continue to be, central to the role of international development institutions and the governments and people they seek to serve.

Notes

1. This can perhaps be connected to the relatively greater influence wielded by one major and environmentally conscious power in these institutions than is the case with other agencies that were examined.

2. It is worth noting that the 1977 review of the OECD Development Assistance Committee (DAC), *Development Co-Operation,* pointed to the same difficulties with respect to "basic needs" programs (see chapter 5, "Some Implications for Donors of a Basic Needs Approach"). It is clearly implicit in the review that the resources needed for the new orientation of the donor countries will primarily be additional to existing aid flows.

3. Ibid., p. 97. Reprinted with permission.

4. In his 1977 address to the World Bank Board of Governors, Bank President Robert McNamara said: "The international community today has no fully adequate analytical mechanism for assessing complex development phenomena and hence no fully adequate means of dealing with them." Robert S. McNamara, *Address to the Board of Governors,* Washington, D.C., September 26, 1977, p. 4. Quoted with permission.

5. See appendix B.

6. Lyn Squire and Herman Van der Tak, *Economic Analysis of Projects,* (Baltimore: Johns Hopkins University Press, 1975).

7. "Measurement of the Health Benefits of Investments in Water Supply," P.U. Report No. 20 (Washington, D.C., International Bank for Reconstruction and Development, 1976). A similar panel has been meeting in the forestry area.

8. Charles Cooper and Robert Otto, "Social and Economic Evaluation of Environmental Impact on Third World Countries," (Social Policy Research Unit (SPRU)/Institute of Development Studies (IDS), 1977). Likewise, members of the academic community have recently joined the discussion. See, for example,

Charles Pearson and Anthony Pryor, *Environment: North and South* (New York: John Wiley and Sons, Ltd., 1978), chapter 4, "Environment and Development Project Appraisal."

9. Examples of such aid exist; for example, the World Bank's rural energy program in Colombia is entirely devoted to the establishment of local institutions; in Liberia and the Congo the World Bank has established training programs for foresters; the UNDP and the World Bank have on occasion provided help with the preparation of national environmental legislation. Many other opportunities for such help undoubtedly exist and would emerge as requests if development financing institutions were to offer their help specifically in these areas.

Appendix A
Aims and Focus of the Study

The target of this study was in part the objective of the United Nations Environment Programme (UNEP) that:

> Guidelines should be elaborated for the integration of the environmental dimension in future development projects, on the basis, *inter alia,* of the assessment of ongoing or completed projects, with an aim of ensuring that the inclusion of environmental parameters does not adversely affect development priorities.[1]

However, the inquiry was not limited to the field defined by the boundaries of a "project" but undertook a general review of the operational functions of the institutions under consideration. The UNEP responsibility "to assist in the formulation of criteria for the evaluation of development projects and their consequences, taking into account the results of planned pilot actions and post-audits" was also considered.[2]

The study was conducted in two phases. The objectives of the first phase were limited to an examination of formal procedures and informal practice across the whole range of funded activities.[3]

The members of the International Institute for Environment and Development (IIED) project team were aware of the controversial and delicate nature of many of the issues involved. In particular, they kept in mind the warning given in 1971 by the Founex meeting of experts on development and environment that:

> ... in the present state of our knowledge there is need for extreme care in devising specific guidelines so that they do not become bottlenecks in the implementation of development projects, or raise such issues in detail as are irrelevant in the current stage of development in many of the developing countries.[4]

The project team was also confronted constantly with the implications for international funding agencies of national sovereignty in the process of project formulation. Again, as the Founex experts stated,

> ... it is for the developing countries to formulate such guidelines in the light of their own experience and requirements ... *No rigid guidelines* should be laid down by multilateral or bilateral donors *at this stage*

unless there has been an opportunity for adequate consultation with the developing countries through various appropriate forums.[5]

But the effort to evaluate the attitudes of multilateral aid institutions towards environmental concern inevitably led to the discussions within the U.N. system of the components of the New International Economic Order. The Charter of Economic Rights and Duties of States asserts:

> The protection, preservation and enhancement of the environment for the present and future generations is the responsibility of all States. All States shall endeavor to establish their own environmental and developmental policies in conformity with such responsibility. The environmental policies of all States should enhance and not adversely affect the present and future development potential of developing countries. All States have the responsibility to ensure that activities within their jurisdiction or control do not cause damage to the environment of other States or of areas beyond the limits of national jurisdiction. All States should cooperate in evolving international norms and regulations in the field of the environment.[6]

This statement was further noted in the various implementing resolutions and declarations which followed. The debate was well summarized by UNEP:

> Today's greatest challenge is to design development so that it satisfies basic needs—but is environmentally realistic and does not transgress the "outer limits" imposed by the capacities of the biosphere.[7]

Project research pursued the line of thought of the authors of the *Cocoyoc Declaration* and of subsequent intergovernmental resolutions regarding meeting the basic needs of the poorest, that:

> The first aim should be to benefit those who need these resources most and to do so in accordance with the principles of solidarity with future generations.[8]

> Conditions should be created for people to learn by themselves through practice how to make the best possible use of the specific resources of the ecosystem in which they live, how to design appropriate technologies, how to organise and educate themselves to this end.[9]

The Action Plan for the Human Environment agreed at Stockholm also recommended that international development agencies:

> . . . be prepared to assist the less industrialised countries in solving the environmental problems of development projects; to this end they

should actively support the training and encourage the recruitment of requisite personnel, as far as possible within these countries themselves.[10]

Instances of where this had occurred were sought throughout the study.

Finally, the IIED team was concerned, as were the governmental authors of the Action Plan, not simply with environmental impact in the sense of pollution or depletion of resources but, as the Action Plan's authors put it, "with the new opportunities that may be offered to ... establish industries and/or expand existing industries in which [developing countries] may have comparative advantage because of environmental considerations."[11]

With the agreement of UNEP and the Canadian International Development Agency (CIDA), who were the financial sponsors of the project, the broad view of the concept of environment was adopted, which is generally assumed now to be the compass of the phrase "environmental management" (see chapter 1). This broad definition differed from the views of funding agency officials who were interviewed.

Scope of the Study

The agencies listed were chosen for inclusion in the study because of their importance in the international funding of development projects, but it was recognized that they had achieved varying levels of regularization of dealing with environmental problems in the course of their work.

African Development Bank (ADB)

Arab Bank for Economic Development of Africa (BADEA)

Asian Development Bank (AsDB)

Caribbean Development Bank (CDB)

European Development Fund (EDF)

Inter-American Development Bank (IDB)

International Bank for Reconstruction and Development (IBRD or World Bank)

Organization of American States (OAS)

United Nations Development Program (UNDP)

The U.N. Development Program (UNDP) and the Organization of American States (OAS) were included, although they are not lending agencies, because their preinvestment feasibility study financing represents a critical phase for environmental assessment and appraisal.

The first phase of the study examined the policies and procedures of these agencies to see whether and to what extent environmental considerations are included within the agencies' broad development goals. This examination included an assessment of each agency's practical perception and definition of environmental considerations, the role which the agencies see for themselves in the promotion of environmental concerns, and the extent to which the agencies will defer to a borrower's determination of its own environmental standards vis-à-vis development goals. In the latter or sectoral part of the study these inquiries were carried into the four fields of development activity described above. As may be imagined, there were great differences among the perceptions of the breadth of what is included in the term "environmental considerations."

Agency environmental assessment guidelines, where they existed, were examined procedurally to assess the role of the assessment program in the overall lending process, and substantively for content and relative specificity. The study's first phase concentrated on an examination of methods which the agencies use to implement environmental assessment activities, while in the sectoral analysis, patterns of lending from an environmental and "basic needs" point of view were examined, as well as the means, if any, that were used to introduce an environmental dimension to sectoral policy. Such mechanisms included environmental assessment studies by the agencies' project proponents and their incorporation into broader feasibility studies, technical assistance on a program or project basis, and financial assistance, on concessionary terms if necessary, for the costs of environmental studies.

Methodology Employed

General Approach

The project team first developed as much background material as possible on the agencies being examined, including historical data, lending patterns, and policies. Background papers summarizing this material were used as briefing documents by those members of the team who visited the agencies. A prospectus describing the project and an indicative questionnaire outlining the kinds of information sought were developed and distributed to agency personnel in advance of interviews.

The project team was divided between the IIED's Washington and London offices. The Washington team, directed by Robert Stein, undertook background research and documentation and conducted interviews with the funding institutions with headquarters in the Western hemisphere. Agencies were visited in New York (UNDP), Washington (IBRD, IDB, and OAS), and Barbados (CDB). The

London team, directed by Brian Johnson, dealt with Abidjan (ADB), Khartoum (Arab Bank for Economic Development of Africa, BADEA), Manila, (AsDB) and Brussels (EDF).

In addition to the efforts of IIED research staff, a group of eight individuals were selected, primarily from the Institute's Board of Directors and Council, who have been consulted on various aspects of the project (see appendix H).

The Interview Process

The initial aim of visits to the nine agencies involved was to develop an understanding of both formal procedures and informal practices for the incorporation of environmental considerations. At the same time, a general picture was developed of what useful initial practical steps could be taken by each agency to improve their environmental assessment work and to ameliorate the environmental impact of their loans and grants.

In addition to documentation on the agencies' organization, procedures, lending processes, and environmental programs, documents on projects of special environmental interest were collected. Special attention was given to project appraisal reports which generally, in the banks visited, are the central documents describing the rationale for loans. In gathering this project documentation special attention was also given to the four selected areas for the second phase of the study: human settlements, water resources (including water supplies, dams, and irrigation), forestry, and energy (with special reference to comparative types of energy sources).

In-depth interviews were conducted within each institution of operations-level personnel charged with the administration of environmental assessment programs, loan officers, policy-level personnel reviewing country economic plans (including individuals responsible for training and project evaluation), and those personnel with broader functions permitting a fuller perspective on the role of environmental assessment in the lending process. The project was discussed with a number of officers and directors in most of the institutions.

The Sectoral Studies

The environmental impact of the policies and procedures established by the lending institutions that were studied must ultimately be measured by the yardstick of operational results.

The project team conducted well over one hundred separate and detailed interviews at the nine institutions, and reviewed much general documentation. In the second phase of the project they evaluated the quality of environmental planning and analysis in specific program areas, or sectors, of development projects. Case studies in the usual sense were not conducted, since it was considered unlikely that a small number of projects would adequately illustrate the approaches taken by these institutions to environmental considerations. Rather, the goal was to uncover a sense of both the recurrent environmental benefits and shortcomings of the practices of the nine institutions in the selected areas.

The four program areas (human settlements, water resource development, forestry, and energy) were chosen for their obvious relevance to meeting basic human needs. They overlap and intersect, so that cross-sectoral planning also came under scrutiny. The exclusion of industrial and many infrastructure sectors from the chosen areas of program study is explained by the relative abundance of knowledge of environmental consequences of development work in these areas. It appeared that a far greater contribution might be made in areas where commonly accepted environmental principles are not widely recognized or applied.

The latter phase of the project looked more deeply into the volume of project documentation collected in the initial round of visits. At this stage sectoral officers and certain loan or project teams were interviewed in greater detail, and further information was collected on those projects within each program area which seemed best to illustrate its de facto standards and practices.

One of the strongest impressions at the completion of the study was the way that this research helped to raise the consciousness of many members of bank staffs interviewed, and appeared to broaden their view of the range of consequences that the term environment could (or should) embrace. In the case of almost every institution visited, the project teams were either asked if they were willing to help with specific recommendations for the incorporation of environmental expertise into the lending process, or to provide consulting services directly. Naturally, such discussions were deferred until after the completion of the project.

Notes

1. United Nations Environment Programme, Governing Council Decisions 8(II) A.1.3(d) and A.II.2(b).
2. Ibid.
3. The objectives of the first-phase study were five-fold:

a. To look at means and procedures established for consideration of alternative approaches to the same project objective, and to review the procedures in operation for preventive or remedial measures for adverse environmental consequences;
b. To study the status and qualifications of funding agencies' personnel

charged with administering environmental assessment programs and the influence that these people bring to bear upon the lending process;

c. To identify gaps in research and practice in these areas;

d. To consider the environmental training needs of recipient country counterpart staff involved in the project negotiation process; and,

e. To examine and compare the means by which environmental costs and benefits of development projects financed by some multilateral development agencies are incorporated into the overall project cost/benefit analysis.

4. Founex Report, para. 46, as in Annex 1, *Development and Environment, UN Conference on the Human Environment, A.CONF.48/10,* 22 December 1971.

5. Ibid.

6. United Nations, General Assembly, *Charter of Economic Rights and Duties of States,* Resolution 3281 (XXIX) chapter 3, article 30.

7. United Nations Environment Programme, 1975, *Annual Review by the Executive Director,* p. 4.

8. UNEP/UNCTAD Symposium, *The Cocoyoc Declaration,* adopted October 12, 1974, p. 9.

9. Ibid., p. 11.

10. U.N. General Assembly, *Report of the United Nations Conference on the Human Environment held at Stockholm, 5-16 June, 1972.* A/CONF.48/14, 3 July 1972, Recommendation 1b, p. 9.

11. Ibid., Recommendation 106b, p. 57.

Appendix B
Methodologies for
Environmental Impact
Appraisal

A growing literature has appeared on environmental economics, mainly concerned with extending the established framework of welfare economics and cost/benefit analysis to deal with environmental matters. For the most part theoretical suggestions have been made; the principles of evaluation are made clear enough, but how to apply them in actual practice is not as clear. So people concerned with project evaluation in practical situations (in planning offices or development banks) are left without much useful guidance.[1]

One of the major problems which economists tend to gloss over is that the economic evaluation of environmental impacts depends upon their being properly specified. Logically this is perhaps so obvious that it is hardly worth saying. In practice it is of the first importance for two reasons. First, because the technical specification of environmental impacts is often very difficult to do. Scientific knowledge in many of these matters is limited: obvious first-order impacts on the physical environment may be easy enough to spot, but second-order impacts are often larger, socially more important, long-term and hard to predict. In addition, there is the technical difficulty that specification of these impacts requires interdisciplinary analysis and is therefore expensive. The second practical aspect is that, as a general rule, departments mainly responsible for economic evaluation of projects hardly ever have the technical skills to specify their impacts and seldom contract outsiders to tell them what the environmental implications will be. This is a huge gap and a serious one. This report has indicated points at which project evaluators could do more to ensure that there is systematic technical specification of environmental impacts. This in itself would be a major step because it would help raise consciousness about the social implications of development projects which at present are too often treated de facto as insignificant, by being largely ignored.

Technical specification is only part of the problem. The evaluation problem remains, which involves some considerable difficulties, especially in producing a monetary measure of environmental damage. Obviously, those concerned with project evaluation want a monetary measure because it would allow commensurability with the more conventional costs and benefits to which they are accustomed. What are the difficulties?

The usual approach to the measurement of project benefits is to determine a society's "willingness to pay" for them. In practical evaluation, the prices of the output of a project are taken as the basic guide to willingness to pay—usually adjusted to deal with particular imperfections in the market, or with the fact that the increase of supply due to the project may change prices. Where a project produces environmental damages, the logically obvious way of measuring the social costs associated with them is to extend the willingness to pay concept, by attempting to find out what people are willing to pay to have the environmental damage abated. This is the textbook approach. It is logical, consistent and, in its own framework, correct, but extremely difficult to implement in practice.

In the first place, there may be no way of establishing a value for environmental impacts. Even if large surveys are done, there are some categories of cost that the people consulted might find extraordinarily difficult to evaluate. At the extreme, people cannot put a monetary value on life itself (measurements of the value of life in cost/benefit analysis are mostly nonsense). They may also find it very difficult to value particular dangers to health and amenity *before* those damages to health and amenity are present.

Second, even if it were possible in principle for people to put monetary values—"prices" as it were—on environmental effects, it may be virtually impossible in practice to consult them. The survey costs of finding out how people value their environment may be enormous. The usual economist's answer is to use revealed-preference measures, like measurements of the fall in house values in areas affected by environmental damage. These, however, present tricky practical problems, and are of limited value in societies where many of the relevant values are not reflected in the market. For example, in some developing countries, house values would be useful only in relation to a small minority of the middle-class population in urban areas, where there is a market in housing.

Third, and perhaps most important, many environmental impacts appear or build up only in the long run. Future willingness to pay is exceedingly hard to measure. Future generations, for example, may put a value on the amenity aspects of the environment which is orders of magnitude greater than that which is put on them today. As urbanization develops, population grows and (hopefully) average income increases, and as availability of environmental amenity (open space to take the simplest example) diminishes, the value people put on it is likely to rise very sharply. And if health and well-being are in question, which doubtless they will be, the value of environmental goods will certainly rise sharply, perhaps far more sharply than anyone realizes today. One can get some feel for this by comparing the widespread present concern with environment in both rich and poor countries, with the virtual absence of any explicit general concerns about these matters fifty years ago. Even today, the price of environmental goods is orders of magnitude greater than it was one or two generations ago; in future years it will doubtless be orders of magnitude higher than it is today. Very often it is precisely these future relative prices of environmental goods that are the relevant ones for today's project evaluation, but they are hard to set.

Apart from these difficulties, there are problems of interpreting measurements of willingness to pay, even when they can be established. One of these is widely discussed: the so-called "free-rider" problem. If one asks a person how much he would be willing to pay to abate a general environmental nuisance,[2] he is likely to understate his own willingness, in the hopes that the costs of abatement would be largely borne by his neighbours, to his advantage. But there are often problems especially relevant to developing countries.

In monetary terms, willingness to pay must obviously vary with a person's level of income. Even if an environmental hazard is a danger to life itself, a very poor person might indicate a low subjective willingness to pay because he or she reckons that they must run the risk of survival in return for a prospect of higher income resulting from an environmentally damaging project. The choices at very low levels of income may be very harsh. The trouble with this is that willingness to pay responses, if used as a guide to environmental policy, must inevitably lead to far greater alleviation of damage that affects the richer classes than of damage affecting the poorer—even if the dangers to the poorer classes are survival dangers. Welfare economics has no way of encompassing distributional aspects, and in the case of environmental damages the effect of skewed distribution on valuation may be very considerable. Plainly, willingness to pay measures need to be reinterpreted, or weighted, to deal with such inequalities.

Another difficulty, also particularly severe in developing countries, is that people's pricing or valuation of environmental damage obviously depends on their having proper and complete information about its effects. Smelly effluents from a factory may be just a general nuisance and one may be willing to live with them, but if one knows that they are poisonous as well as smelly, one takes a very different view. The trouble is that environmental impacts are complex (sometimes too complex for environmentalists themselves to work out) so their effects can only be expressed as probabilities. Consequently, conveying information about them to people is expensive and difficult, especially when the media for communication are underdeveloped, as is usually the case in the Third World. And people's responses to such information and their ability to relate to the probabilities of, say a health hazard, often depend on their general levels of education and information. When large parts of the population are substantially unschooled and illiterate, it is especially difficult for them to respond to complex information about environmental damage and it may be hard to simplify the information itself.

A final difficulty of interpretation (special to the Third World) is that people's willingness to pay for abatement of environmental damage is in most cases likely to be reduced if only part of their income is in money; for example, if a significant proportion of income is in food and simple manufactures they produce for their own consumption. If their opportunities for expanding money income as a substitute for subsistence income are few, and if the uses of money income are essential to them, then willingness to pay in money terms to offset environmental damage may be much reduced. The true subjective value of environmental goods to them is thus underestimated.

Beyond these considerable difficulties, there are two other predominantly technical problems. The first is the problem of time—the much discussed difficulties of the "rate of discount" in project evaluation. The argument is that environmental costs are often most significant in the long-run, and that the use of a discount rate to reduce these long-run costs to a present value results in their having a nearly negligible weight in the evaluation of projects. This problem can be overstated. Project evaluators should be concerned, not only with the present value of the project in its starting year (the starting condition), but also with its net present value in each year of operation (the continuation decision). If there are heavy environmental costs in the longer run, they drastically affect the viability of a project, even though its net present value is very high (that is, the starting condition is met). However, since project evaluations seldom explicitly consider the continuation decision (that is, the condition that the project should only be continued for so long as its net present value for the remainder of its economic life is positive), many projects with large long-run environmental costs probably are wrongly initiated.[3]

The second technical problem is that project evaluation techniques are designed mainly for economically marginal projects, though they are frequently applied to nonmarginal situations. This presents two sorts of problems from the environmental point of view. On the one hand, a good proportion of environmental damage probably arises from projects which are nonmarginal in narrower economic terms. On the other hand, projects which are marginal in narrow terms may produce environmental impacts which are nonmarginal. Allied to this is the problem that, if the environmental impacts occur in the long run, changes in demand and supply for environmental goods (such as have been discussed) will produce nonmarginalities. One response to problems of nonmarginality has been to develop mean economic models to examine the economy-wide implications of nonmarginal projects, for example, the extended use of input-output analysis. Unfortunately, these are expensive and do not escape from the underlying problems of valuation. In other words, they do not provide a solution to the problem of how to put a price on the environment, which is the problem project evaluators would most like to solve.

This is a rather formidable list of difficulties, none of which is easily resolved. However, in an immediate practical sense, the question is not so much how to solve the technical problems of evaluation, but how to respond to them, while recognizing that they are there and unsolved. What to do about it?

It seems desirable to make four points which underlie the precise proposals which follow.

The first is that all investment projects by definition have environmental impacts and most (though not all) of these impacts are unpriced; in other words they do not appear in the valuations that are commonly used in project assessment. These unvalued impacts are often very important in their implications for amenity, health and welfare (in the broad sense of quality of life), and sometimes for future production, too. It is now also quite clear that such unpriced environmental impacts in the Third World affect not merely the comfort of the comparatively rich, but also—more often than might be recognized—the physical survival and life expectancies of the very poor.

Second, project evaluators in development banks are not alone in having paid comparatively little attention to the detailed environmental impacts of projects and their long-run social implications. Reluctance to deal with these matters is natural in professional activities where putting prices on things is de rigueur. However, as every project evaluator would agree, the fact that it is very difficult to find out the price of environmental goods, does not mean one does not exist, nor does it preclude the social cost of environmental impacts from being high. Perhaps the problem is that too little attention has been given in development banks, as elsewhere, to the proper technical specification of environmental impacts. Often when they are specified more fully, and their likely effects on individuals and societies spelled out, the problem of pricing them may appear somewhat secondary, as it becomes obvious that something must be done to respond to them.

Third, because of the valuation problems (and the constraints imposed by requirements of financial viability as opposed to economic viability in a broader social sense) development banks, like other financing agencies, have found it difficult to use cost/benefit methodology to justify projects whose main purpose is simply environmental improvement. However, environmental improvement, particularly among the rural poor, may have very considerable economic value, and often in the long run, may make a contribution to growth of output.

Fourth, many of the problems discussed here cannot be solved by development banks. For example, it is obviously desirable that the mass of people should have fuller information about the impacts on their environment—particularly that the poor and illiterate should have much more knowledge of these matters. It is equally desirable that the lack of knowledge and information among the mass of people should not lead to judgments about what is environmentally desirable being preempted by purely technocratic decision-making. Political institutions are needed that will not only allow, but encourage, popular participation in decisions about how to deal with environmental threats or environmental preservation. In many countries new institutions will be needed. In some poor countries, with their special problems of large masses of poor, illiterate, and badly informed rural people whose environmental problems may affect survival, the need for institutional experiments is especially urgent. Any institutional response along these lines will have to face the fact that environmental issues very often involve questions of distribution of welfare, and so are political in an important and unavoidable sense.

There is little that the development banks can do about such questions because they are so obviously questions of national policy. But the banks should respond, perhaps, to the fact that the needed kind of institution does not exist for the most part, so people's preferences about their environment are largely unexpressed. This puts a special responsibility about the matter on agencies who influence investment decisions which affect the environment.

What more precise proposals can be made? The following responses suggest themselves:

1. Much more attention should be paid to the systematic specification of environmental impacts, within the unfortunately narrow limits that scientific knowledge will allow. The second-order effects of environmental impacts (especially cumulative, long-run effects) are obviously particularly important. The likely social implications of environmental impacts should be systematically described.

2. Project evaluators should not give up attempts to quantify environmental impacts. The difficulties of pricing are sometimes insuperable (because willingness to pay is often unknowable), but not always. Some environmental impacts may mostly influence future production, and these can be specified. However, any valuations need to be treated with caution. Particular care is necessary with distortions that may arise from inadequate information, distributional effects of damage, and problems of valuation by people whose income is only partly monetary.

3. If monetary valuation is impossible, project evaluators must judge the relative economic importance of environmental impacts. Ranking procedures may help here, but it is important to remember that ranking environmental effects is no more than a systematic way of making value judgments. Ranking, particularly weighted ranking which is often used to gauge environmental damage, is no more than a pricing procedure in itself, the prices being determined by experts. The danger of this kind of pricing by technical experts is that it may leave socially relevant considerations out of account (for example, distributional effects). Criteria for ranking, and more generally for making value judgments, must be clear.

4. Environmental standards are established in many fields in a number of countries. In the absence of adequate measures of valuation, they are critically necessary, and project evaluation should be done within a framework of standards. However, there are many crucial areas where standards do not exist, or perhaps cannot be drawn up. Some of these areas are particularly important in the Third World, such as the impacts of overgrazing and soil depletion. The absence of standards in these areas can be a danger. The fact that a project meets specified standards should not mean ipso facto that it is acceptable on environmental grounds. Another special problem is that standards are generally specific to advanced country climates, physical, and animal life environments: Third World environments may be more vulnerable to certain types of damage and would need special standards. So an unthinking use of standards poses its own dangers.

5. There remain very major difficulties in dealing with long-run environ-

mental effects. The main one is that the benefits of a sound physical environment may have steeply increasing relative prices as population grows and pressure on resources grows with it. It is hard to estimate how the next generation will value the choice between increased material income and the physical environment. It is, however, a safe bet that physical environment will be favored much more than it is today. Because of the uncertainties about future valuations of the environment and particularly where the risks to health and life are significant, long-run environmental considerations could be discounted at specially low rates—often zero. This is one way of dealing with uncertainties about future relative values. Another approach is to assign values to environmental benefits which predict their increasing value over time, and to insert these larger values into the benefit stream, discounting them as usual. If either of these methods tends to err on the side of environmental conservation—if indeed that can be described as an error—it is a more rational direction for error than the alternative.

6. Nonmarginality is a major problem also largely unresolved. Project evaluators can only respond to it in a limited way for the present—namely, by making sure they have specified all the intersectoral production effects of a new investment, so that their environmental consequences can be assessed. Increased paper production not only produces a great deal of effluent in its own right, but may also deplete forest reserves, with the well-known and very negative effects this can have. Linkages like this are obviously critical. More sophisticated input-output approaches may be helpful in national policy-making, but they are not yet very helpful for project evaluators in development banks. Their data needs are enormous, and especially in the Third World, the data is usually not available and would cost a great deal to generate.

Notes

1. Some staff in the banks believe that the data requirements of the new methodologies are too complex to be used by development planners. Less academically rigorous techniques, such as weighting benefits, have been advocated so that benefits to poorer people are counted more heavily than benefits to richer classes. There is a corresponding theory of weighting costs according to income distribution criteria, a practice of great significance because environmental costs are often most heavily borne by the poor. The use of sensitivity analysis on projects to see if relatively minor changes (environmental or other) in assumptions will have a significant bearing on anticipated economic return is a third technique. A few project planners have been more careful of late to evaluate the costs of not doing a project (the with/without condition), especially in forestry, land reclamation, and irrigation projects. All of these informal approaches deserve further consideration and support, but the use of these

admittedly second-best alternatives should not arrest the search for more exact techniques.

2. The answer would only have meaning if he believes he would have to pay some amount which depended on his answer. If he believed "the government will pay" out of tax revenues, his answer would not reflect his subjective evaluation of the environmental damage.

3. C.M. Cooper and R. Otto, "Social and Economic Evaluation of Environmental Impacts in Third World Countries," (Social Policy Research Unit/Institute of Development Studies: Mimeo), 1977; and C.M. Cooper, "A Note on the Evaluation of Projects with Long-term Social Costs," (SPRU/IDS: Mimeo), 1977.

Appendix C
Memberships of the Organizations Included in the Study

The African Development Bank

Algeria	Malawi
Benin	Mali
Botswana	Mauritania
Burundi	Mauritius
Cameroons	Morocco
Cape Verde Islands	Mozambique
Central African Empire	Niger
Chad	Nigeria
Comoros	Rwanda
Congo, People's Republic of	Sao Tome e Principe
Egypt, Arab Republic of	Seychelles
Equatorial Guinea	Senegal
Ethiopia	Sierra Leone
Gabon	Somalia
Gambia, The	Sudan, The
Ghana	Swaziland
Guinea	Tanzania
Guinea-Bissau	Togo
Ivory Coast	Tunisia
Kenya	Uganda
Lesotho	Upper Volta
Liberia	Zaire
Libya	Zambia
Madagascar	

The African Development Fund

Consists of all the members of the African Development Bank and:

Belgium	Finland
Brazil	France
Canada	Germany, Federal Republic of
Denmark	Italy

Japan   Sweden
Kuwait   Switzerland
Netherlands   United Kingdom
Norway   United States
Saudi Arabia   Yugoslavia
Spain

The Arab Bank for Economic Development of Africa

Algeria   Morocco
Bahrain   Oman
Egypt, Arab Republic of   Palestine Liberation Organization
Iraq   Qatar
Jordan   Saudi Arabia
Kuwait   Sudan, The
Lebanon   Syrian Arab Republic
Libya   Tunisia
Mauritania   United Arab Emirates

The Asian Development Bank

Afghanistan   Lao People's Democratic Republic
Australia   Malaysia
Austria   Maldives
Bangladesh   Netherlands
Belgium   Nepal
Burma   New Zealand
Canada   Norway
China, Republic of   Pakistan
Cook Islands   Papua New Guinea
Democratic Kampuchea   Philippines
Denmark   Singapore
Fiji   Sri Lanka
Finland   Solomon Islands
France   Sweden
Germany, Federal Republic of   Switzerland
Gilbert Islands   Thailand
Hong Kong   Tonga
India   United Kingdom
Indonesia   United States
Italy   Viet Nam, Socialist Republic of
Japan   Western Samoa
Korea, Republic of

The Caribbean Development Bank

Regional states and territories:

Antigua	Guyana
Bahamas	Jamaica
Barbados	Montserrat
Belize	St. Kitts/Nevis/Anguilla
British Virgin Islands	St. Lucia
Cayman Islands	St. Vincent
Colombia	Trinidad and Tobago
Dominican Republic	Turks and Caicos Islands
Grenada	Venezuela

Nonregional states:

Canada
United Kingdom

The World Bank (The International Bank for Reconstruction and Development)

Afghanistan	Colombia
Algeria	Comoros*
Argentina	Congo, People's Republic of the
Australia	Costa Rica
Austria	Cyprus
Bahamas*	Democratic Kampuchea
Bahrain*	Denmark
Bangladesh	Dominican Republic
Barbados*	Ecuador
Belgium	Egypt, Arab Republic of
Bolivia	El Salvador
Botswana	Equatorial Guinea
Brazil	Ethiopia
Burma	Fiji
Burundi	Finland
Cameroon	France
Canada	Gabon
Central African Empire	Gambia, The
Chad	Germany, Federal Republic of
Chile	Ghana
China	Greece

*These countries are members of the World Bank but not the International Development Association.

Grenada
Guatemala
Guinea
Guinea-Bissau
Guyana
Haiti
Honduras
Iceland
India
Indonesia
Iran
Iraq
Ireland
Israel
Italy
Ivory Coast
Jamaica*
Japan
Jordan
Kenya
Korea
Kuwait
Lao People's Democratic Republic
Lebanon
Lesotho
Liberia
Libya
Luxembourg
Madagascar
Malawi
Malaysia
Mali
Mauritania
Mauritius
Mexico
Morocco
Nepal
Netherlands
New Zealand
Nicaragua
Niger
Nigeria
Norway

Oman
Pakistan
Panama
Papua New Guinea
Paraguay
Peru
Philippines
Portugal*
Qatar*
Romania*
Rwanda
Saudi Arabia
Senegal
Sierra Leone
Singapore*
Somalia
South Africa
Spain
Sri Lanka
Sudan, The
Swaziland
Sweden
Syrian Arab Republic
Tanzania
Thailand
Togo
Trinidad and Tobago
Tunisia
Turkey
Uganda
United Arab Emirates*
United Kingdom
United States
Upper Volta
Uruguay*
Venezuela*
Viet Nam
Western Samoa
Yemen Arab Republic
Yemen, People's Democratic Republic of
Yugoslavia
Zaire
Zambia

*These countries are members of the World Bank but not the International Development Association.

The European Development Fund

Member states:

Belgium	Italy
Denmark	Luxembourg
France	Netherlands
Germany, Federal Republic of	United Kingdom
Ireland	

The EDF lends to African/Caribbean/Pacific states of:

Bahamas	Madagascar
Barbados	Malawi
Benin	Mali
Botswana	Mauritania
Cameroon	Mauritius
Cape Verde Islands	Niger
Central African Empire	Nigeria
Chad	Papua New Guinea
Comoros	Rwanda
Congo, People's Republic of the	Sao Tome e Principe
Djibouti	Senegal
Equatorial Guinea	Seychelles
Ethiopia	Sierra Leone
Fiji	Somalia
Gabon	Sudan, The
Gambia, The	Surinam
Ghana	Swaziland
Grenada	Tanzania
Guinea	Togo
Guinea-Bissau	Tonga
Guyana	Trinidad and Tobago
Ivory Coast	Uganda
Jamaica	Upper Volta
Kenya	Western Samoa
Lesotho	Zaire
Liberia	Zambi

The Inter-American Development Bank

Argentina	Bolivia
Austria	Brazil
Barbados	Canada
Belgium	Chile

Colombia   Mexico
Costa Rica   Nicaragua
Denmark   Panama
Dominican Republic   Paraguay
Ecuador   Peru
El Salvador   Spain
Guatemala   Switzerland
Guyana   Trinidad and Tobago
Haiti   United Kingdom
Honduras   United States
Israel   Uruguay
Jamaica   Venezuela
Japan   Yugoslavia

The Organization of American States

Argentina   Haiti
Barbados   Honduras
Bolivia   Jamaica
Brazil   Mexico
Colombia   Nicaragua
Costa Rica   Panama
Cuba*   Paraguay
Chile   Peru
Dominican Republic   Surinam
Ecuador   Trinidad and Tobago
El Salvador   United States
Grenada   Uruguay
Guatemala   Venezuela

The United Nations Development Programme

All members of the United Nations and the United Nations system of Specialised
Agencies are members of the United Nations Development Programme.

---

*The people of Cuba, not the government, are a member of the OAS.

**Appendix D
Basic Information on
the Institutions Studied**

Organization	Date of Founding	Location	Professional Staff Size	Member States (Nonregional)
International Bank for Reconstruction and Development	1945 (IDA-1960)	Washington, D.C. U.S.A.	5,000 (approx.) (1978)	129 (IDA-117)
Inter-American Development Bank	1959	Washington, D.C. U.S.A.	900 (approx.) (1977)	37/(14)
Asian Development Bank	1966	Manila Philippines	296 (1977)	43/(13)
Caribbean Development Bank	1968	Bridgetown Barbados	56 (1976)	20/(2)
Organization of American States (Dept. Regional Devel.)	1945 1973	Washington, D.C. U.S.A.	780 (1975)	26
United Nations Development Programme	1950 U.S.A.	New York, N.Y.	567 (1976)	149
European Development Fund	1958	Brussels Belgium	130 (approx.)[a] (1978)	9 (lends to 52 ACP countries[b])
African Development Bank	1964 (ADF-1973)	Abidjan Ivory Coast	101 (1976)	66/(19)
Arab Bank for Economic Development of Africa	1975	Khartoum Sudan	32 (1977)	18

[a]Represents roughly 80 percent of professional staff in the Directorate General for Development.
[b]States which are parties to the Lomé Convention.

**Appendix E
Lending Operations of
the Institutions Studied**

Organization	Total # Projects	Total U.S. $millions	Lending 1972-1976 # Projects	Lending 1972-1976 U.S. $millions
World Bank				
Bank (1946-1977)	1,453	38,610	513	16,532
IDA (1960-1977)	666	11,397	353	6,683
Total	2,119	50,007	866	23,215
Inter-American Development Bank (1961-1976)	975	10,222	313	5,705
Asian Development Bank (1968-1977)	309	4,246	205	2,726
Caribbean Development Bank (1970-1976)	243	111.3	224	105.6
African Development Bank (1967-1976)	177	624.7	153	566.3
Arab Bank for Economic Development of Africa (1975-1977)	23	147.5	23	147.5
United Nations Development Program[a] (1972976)		1,655	—	1,655
Organization of American States[b] (1970-1975)		101.5	—	92.0 (1971-75)
European Development Fund[c] (1959-1977)		3,376	—	1,203(1974-77)

[a]First country programming cycle expenditures.

[b]Net direct services.

[c]All commitments including: grants, loans, risk capital, and compensatory financing.

Appendix F
Loans and Grants by
Sector

	Totals U.S. $Mn.	% Ag.	% Ind.	% Water	% Urban	% Educ.	% Power	% Trans. & Comm.	% Other
IBRD									
1946-77	50,008.1	20.8	8.3	3.3	1.0	3.7	18.8	26.5	9.8
1977	7,066.8	32.7	10.4	4.3	2.2	4.1	13.5	16.8	16.1
IDB									
1961-76	10,222	24	15	9	5	4	20	18	5
1976	1,528	28	20	8	3	5	14	16	6
AsDB									
1968-77	4,245.9	24.7	21.4	9.8	.5	1.1	23.4	18.9	—
1977	865.9	27.6	15.9	9.8	2.4	2.3	25.1	16.9	—
CDB									
1970-76	111.3	23.3	17.2	4.6	12.0	0.9	3.2	36.2	2.6
1976	25.16	15.5	17.0	13.0	23.1	0.9	4.1	26.2	0.2

	Totals U.S. $Mn.	% Ag.	% Ind.	% Health	% Social Welfare	% Educ.	% Plann.	% Trans. & Comm.	% Other
UNDP									
1976 all appr.	5,109	27.9	20.6	6.2	2.6	14.4	11.3	11.3	5.7
1976 expendit.	1,655	27.8	21.7	5.8	2.2	12.2	13.1	12.4	4.8

	Totals U.S. $Mn.	% Tech. Assist.	% Equip.	% Support Action	% Basic Studies	% Train.	% Reg. Action
OAS							
1970-75	101.5	41.9	5.7	6.8	3.0	36.6	—
1975	24.9	49.4	—	—	—	26.1	24.5

EDF		% Ag.	% Ind.	% Health	Water & Housing	% Educ.	% Trans. & Comm.	% Other
1959-73	1,926	28.5	4.6	4.4	6.6	12.8	37.3	5.5
1969-73	637.7	29.6	7.1	0.9	4.7	10.4	37.5	9.7

ADB		% Ag.	% Ind.	% Educ. & Health	% Public Utilit.	% Trans.
1967-76	406.6	11.5	22.2	—	34.6	31.7
1976	90.1	13.9	14.5	11.1	38.9	21.6

BADEA		% Ag.	% Ind.	% Water	% Power	% Infra-structure
1975-76	143.6	20.5	12.6	9.7	10.4	46.8
1976	62.0	28.8	—	—	24.2	47.0

Appendix G
The Project Cycle

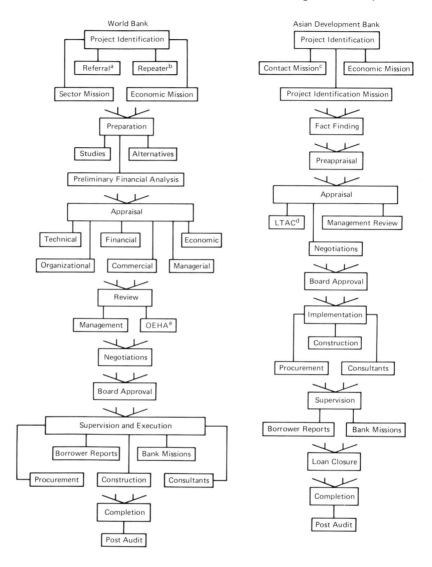

Sources: Adapted from Baum, Warren C., "The Project Cycle" in *Finance and Development* (Washington, IBRD, June 1970), and Asian Development Bank, "Questions and Answers" (Manila, AsDB, April 1977).

[a]Referral projects are those brought forward by new borrowers interested in having bank assistance.

[b]Repeater loans are given to a past borrower for subsequent stages of development of the same or a similar project.

[c]Contact missions are sent regularly to developing member countries for discussions with the authorities concerned.

[d]LTAC is the Loan and Technical Assistance Coordinating Committee.

[e]OEHA is the Office of Environmental and Health Affairs.

Appendix H
Project Advisory Group

The following individuals, largely drawn from the International Institute for Environment and Development Board and Council, were solicited to help define the project and to contribute their expertise in the fields of developmental aspects of environment.

Gerardo Budowski (Costa Rica), Director of Forestry Department, Centro Agronomica Tropical de Investigacion y Ensenanza; former Secretary-General of the International Union for the Conservation of Nature and Natural Resources, Morges, Switzerland.

Carlos Chagas (Brazil), biophysicist; member of the United Nations Advisory Committee on Science and Technology; Director, Instituto Biofisica.

Robert Gardiner (Ghana), Commissioner for Economic Planning, Ghana; former executive secretary, United Nations Economic Commission for Africa.

Felipe Herrera (Chile), well-known economist; former president, Inter-American Development Bank.

Mohamed Kassas (Egypt), professor, University of Cairo; Assistant Director, Arab League Education, Cultural and Scientific Organization; vice president, SCOPE.

Soedjatmoko (Indonesia), Director of Indonesian Planning Agency; member of the Board of Trustees, Ford Foundation; former Ambassador from Indonesia to the United States.

Otto Soemarwoto (Indonesia), professor of bio-management, University of Padjadjaran, Indonesia.

Victor Urquidi (Mexico), President, El Colegio de Mejico; member of The Club of Rome; prominent educator.

Appendix I
International Institute
for Environment and
Development
Assessment Project
Team

Codirectors
Brian Johnson
Robert E. Stein

Project Staff
Stuart Donelson
R. Thomas Hoffmann

Consultants
Robert O. Blake, Senior Fellow
Charles Cooper
George Francis
Peter Freeman
Jorge Hardoy, Senior Fellow
Ralph Luken
Susana Schkolnik

Support Staff
Elizabeth Billings
Mae Dell Dulaney
Hertha Hanu
Tina Kimes
Jeffrey Lee
Francine Spencer
Lisa Martinez Take

Appendix J
Environmental Assessment Program of the International Institute for Environment and Development—A Brief Overview

This study of multilateral development assistance organizations is the first in a series of planned activities that comprise the environmental assessment program of the International Institute for Environment and Development (IIED). This program aims to convey the importance of environmental awareness and procedures to a variety of groups, including the following:

1. Officials in multilateral and bilateral development assistance agencies of donor countries.

2. Environmental experts concerned more directly with development, including, in particular, operational staff of aid agencies and national development ministries, whose work could have an important influence on the environmental dimension of development projects.

3. Officials of governments of developing countries which draw on the funds of these organizations.

4. Agencies within donor governments that are concerned with the development process.

5. Citizen groups; environment- or development-oriented private organizations; and, largely through the media, the public.

The proposed program aims at these particular audiences because the cumulative impact of reaching all of them could accomplish three objectives. First, the involvement and commitment of governments in developing countries to environmentally sound development of their human and natural resources is, and must be, an important objective of IIED's assessment program. The second objective involves directly improving the environmental work of the aid institutions and other involved organizations. The agencies are worldwide leaders in the development field, and it is surely time that they fully recognize the responsibilities of that position.

The third objective of the program is to catalyze the concern and involvement of as many organizations and individuals as possible. Whenever possible, IIED will solicit the active support or cosponsorship of other like-minded organizations. In this way, it will be possible not just to disseminate IIED's views, but to create an informal network of research organizations and citizen groups who will take up similar and related issues. Indeed, the foundations of such a network have already been set out in the concept of locating affiliated project teams to conduct aspects of the research in the upcoming study of bilateral aid agencies.

The first step is the present multilateral study. As a second step, the IIED is evaluating the work of the aid agencies of the United States, the United Kingdom, Canada, the Netherlands, Sweden, and the Federal Republic of Germany. Some of the agencies are leaders in establishing new development policies, and all have lessons to learn from the others. This new study will take eighteen months, and is codirected by Robert O. Blake in the IIED's Washington office, and Brian Johnson in London.

To carry out the proposed inquiry the IIED has initiated coordinated research into the environmental practices and procedures of the aid agency in each of the countries to be included in the study. IIED has selected and is working with affiliated project teams in most or all of the countries involved. Each affiliate will, in association with the IIED assessment project team, carry out much of the actual research on the bilateral aid program in its country.

IIED is also developing plans for two additional projects. One would be a study of environmental attitudes and policies in a small, representative group of developing countries, one on each of the main southern continents. It would analyze the national, cultural, social, and economic background to environmental attitudes and policies. It would identify sources of environmental concern and expertise, both governmental and nongovernmental, and it would study their interaction. The study would focus on the period since preparations for the first World Environment Conference (Stockholm, 1972) when official cognizance was first formally taken by many national governments of environmental issues, and when national reports on the state of the environment were prepared for the UN Secretariat. It is contemplated that the methodology for this project would again involve the use of local research teams.

The other activity planned for the near future responds directly to one of the conclusions of *Banking on the Biosphere?* IIED is organizing a panel and working group of experts in the field of project appraisal methodology, to propose practical alternative forms of analysis and accountancy for including long-term social and environmental effects of projects. Their research will consider the problem of how to refine existing project appraisal methodologies and propose additional tests to give environmental factors their due weight in the decision-making process.

Appendix K
Glossary of
Abbreviations

ACP   African, Caribbean, and Pacific states signing agreement with nine members of the European Community in 1975 Lome Convention.

ADB   African Development Bank.

ADBUA   African Development Bank Unit of Account

ADF   African Development Fund.

AsDB   Asian Development Bank.

BADEA   Arab Bank for Economic Development of Africa.

CDB   Caribbean Development Bank.

CEM   Country Economic Missions, carried out by the World Bank.

CIDA   Canadian International Development Agency.

CPS   Central Project Staff, Office of Environmental and Health Affairs, World Bank.

DAC   Development Assistance Committee, Organization for Economic Cooperation and Development (OECD).

ECOSOC   Economic and Social Council, United Nations.

EDF   European Development Fund.

EEC   European Economic Community.

ESCAP   Economic and Social Commission for Asia and the Pacific, Housing and Technology Division, United Nations.

EUA   European Units of Account.

FAO   Food and Agriculture Organization, United Nations.

FUA   Fund Units of Account.

IAEA   International Atomic Energy Agency, United Nations.

IBRD   International Bank for Reconstruction and Development (or World Bank).

ICRISAT   International Crop Research Institute for Semi-Arid Tropics.

IDA   International Development Association, World Bank.

IDB   Inter-American Development Bank.

IFC   International Finance Corporation.

IIED   International Institute for Environment and Development.

IITA   International Institute of Tropical Agriculture.

OAPEC   Organization of Arab Petroleum Exporting Countries.

OAS   Organization of American States.

OECD   Organization for Economic Cooperation and Development.

OEHA   Office of Environmental and Health Affairs, World Bank.

PAHO   Pan American Health Organization.

PRD   Program of Regional Development, Secretariat for Economic and Social Affairs, Organization of American States.

SCOPE Scientific Committee on Problems of the Environment.

SPTF Social Progress Trust Fund, of which the Inter-American Development Bank was the administrator.

TAD Technical Advisory Division, United Nations Development Programme.

UA Units of Account.

UNDP United Nations Development Programme.

UNEP United Nations Environment Programme.

UNESCO United Nations Educational, Scientific and Cultural Organization.

USAID United States Agency for International Development.

USERDA United States Energy, Research and Development Administration.

WHO World Health Organization.

Bibliography

Books

Acheson, A.L.K.; Chant, J.F.; and Prachoung, M.F.J., eds. *Bretton Woods Revisited.* New York: Macmillan and Co., 1972.

American Society of Civil Engineers. *Environmental Impacts of International Civil Engineering Projects and Practices.* Washington: American Society of Civil Engineers, 1977.

Brown, Lester. *The Twenty-Ninth Day.* New York: W.W. Norton and Co., 1978.

Dasmann, Raymond E.; Milton, John P.; and Freeman, Peter H. *Ecological Principles for Economic Development.* New York: John Wiley and Sons, 1973.

Dell, Sidney Samuel. *The Inter-American Development Bank: A Study in Development Financing.* New York: Praeger Publishers, 1972.

Eckholm, Erik. *Losing Ground: Environmental Stress and World Food Prospects.* New York: W.W. Norton and Co., 1976.

Farvar, M. Taghi, and Milton, John P., eds. *The Careless Technology: Ecology and International Development.* New York: The National History Press, 1972.

Giddman, Charles R.; McEvoy, James, III; and Richardson, Peter J.; eds. *Environmental Quality and Water Development.* San Francisco: W.H. Freeman and Co., 1973.

Hayes, Denis. *Rays of Hope: The Transition to a Post-Petroleum World.* New York: W.W. Norton and Co., 1977.

Lamson-Scribner, Frank H., Jr., ed. *Industrial Project Analysis: Case Studies.* Washington: Economic Development Institute of the World Bank, January 1977.

Mason, Edward S., and Asher, Robert E. *The World Bank Since Bretton Woods.* Cambridge, Mass.: Ballinger Publishing Co., 1973.

Pearson, Charles, and Pryor, Anthony. *Environment North and South: An Economic Interpretation.* New York: John Wiley and Sons, 1978.

Pearson, Lester B. *Partners in Development: Report of the Commission on International Development.* New York: Praeger Publishers, 1969.

Saunders, Robert and Warford, Jeremy. *Village Water Supply.* Washington: International Bank for Reconstruction and Development, 1977.

Swainson, Neil A., ed. *Managing the Water Environment.* Vancouver: University of British Columbia Press, 1976.

Squire, Lyn, and Van der Tak, Herman G. *Economic Analysis of Projects.* Baltimore: Johns Hopkins Press, 1975.

Ward, Barbara. *The Home of Man.* New York: W.W. Norton and Co., 1976.

White, Gilbert F.; Bradley, David J.; and White, Anne U. *Drawers of Water: Domestic Use in East Africa.* Chicago: University of Chicago Press, 1972.

Periodicals

Applebaum, George D. "Controlling the Environmental Hazards of International Development." *Ecology Law Quarterly,* vol. 5, no. 2 (1976):321-76.
"Bulletin of the European Communities: Environment Programme." 1977-1981.
"Environmental Activities of Development Assistance Agencies." *SAIS REVIEW,* vol. 18, no. 3 (1976):14-23.
Ewing, A.F. "Pre-Investment." *Journal of World Trade Law,* vol. 8, no. 3, (May-June 1974):316-328.
Friedmann, Efrain. "Financing Energy in Development Countries." *Energy Policy* (March 1976).
Geoghegan, Michael. "Third World and Global Society: A Case Study on the Origins of the United Nations Development Programme." *Unified World,* nos. 3, 4, 5 (May, June, July, 1976). New York: New World Forum, 1976.
"A Growing Worry: The Consequences of Development." *Conservation Foundation Letter.* January 1978.
Human Settlements. New York: Center for Housing, Building, and Planning, vols. 2-7 (1972-77).
Joyner, Christopher C., and Joyner, Nancy D. "Global Eco-Management and International Organizations: The Stockholm Conference and Problems of Cooperation." *Natural Resources Journal,* vol. 14, no. 4 (October 1974):533-66.
Page, T., et al. "Drinking Water and Cancer Mortality in Louisiana." *Science,* vol. 193 (1976):55.
Revelle, Roger. "The Resources Available for Agriculture." *Scientific American,* vol. 235, no. 3 (1976):165-78.
The Urban Edge. Washington, D.C.: Council for International Urban Liaison, vol. 1, nos. 1-5.

Reports and Papers

Anstee, Margaret Joan. *The Administration of International Development Aid.* Syracuse: Maxwell School of Citizenship and Public Affairs, 1969.
Arnow, Ted. *Reconnaissance of Dam and Reservoir Sites in the Upper Rio Bermejo Basin, Argentina.* Washington: U.S. Geological Survey, December 1971.
Banco Nacional de Comercio Exterior. *Ecodesarrollo: Cuarto Ensayos.* Mexico City: Banco Nacional de Comercio Exterior, 1976.
Bene, J.G.; Beall, H.W.; and Cote, A. *Trees, Food and People: Land Management in the Tropics.* Ottawa: International Development Research Centre, 1977.
Berthelot, Roger M. *Jonglei Canal: UNDP Fact-Finding Mission Report.* United Nations Development Programme: February 1976.

Bigelow, Charles D. *Capital Financing for Development in the Context of the Human Environment: An African Case.* U.N. Conference on the Human Environment, Stockholm, Sweden, June 1972.

The Cocoyoc Declaration. United Nations Environment Programme (UNEP)/ United Nations Conference on Trade and Development (UNCTAD) Symposium on Patterns of Resource Use, Environment and Development Strategies, Cocoyoc, Mexico, 8-12 October 1974.

Comptroller General of the United States. *Conservation Practices Applied Relative to Three Foreign Development Projects Supported by World Bank Loans.* (prepared at the request of Henry S. Reuss, U.S. House of Representatives), Washington, D.C.: GAO, April 1974 (B-161470).

Conference on the Human Environment Secretariat. *Development and Environment (Subject Area V).* Conference on the Human Environment, Stockholm, Sweden, June 5-16, 1972. General Assembly Document A/Conf. 48/10.

Cooper, Charles, and Robert Otto. "Social and Economic Evaluation of Environmental Impact on Third World Countries." Unpublished paper. University of Sussex: Institute of Development Studies/SPRU, 1977.

Democratic Republic of the Sudan, Executive Organ for Development Projects in the Jonglei Area. *Jonglei Project (Phase One).* Khartoum: January 1975.

Dworkin, Daniel, M., ed. *Environmental Sciences in Developing Countries. Report no. 4, Indianapolis, Indiana: SCOPE, 1974.*

_____. *Environment and Development,* Indianapolis, Indiana: Scientific Committee on Problems of the Environment (SCOPE), 1974.

Eckholm, Erik. *The Other Energy Crisis: Firewood.* Worldwatch Paper 1, Washington, D.C.: Worldwatch Institute, September 1975.

Eckholm, Erik, and Brown, Lester R. *Spreading Deserts: The Hand of Man.* Worldwatch Paper 13, Washington, D.C.: Worldwatch Institute, August 1977.

Environment Training Programme (ENDA). *Environment and Development: Research, Education and Training Geared Toward Action.* Occasional Paper no. 77-14, Supplement to *African Environment: Environmental Studies and Regional Planning Bulletin.* Dakar, Senegal: March 1977.

Founex Report. *Report of a Panel of Experts Convened by the Secretary-General of the United Nations Conference on the Human Environment* (Founex, Switzerland, June 4-12, 1971). In *Development and Environment* (A/CONF.48/10). December 22, 1971.

Fox, Robert. *Urban Population Growth Trends in Latin America.* Washington, D.C.: Inter-American Development Bank, 1975.

Freeman, Peter H. *Large Dams and the Environment.* Washington, D.C.: International Institute for Environment and Development, 1977.

_____. *The Environmental Impact of a Large Tropical Reservoir: Guidelines for Policy and Planning* (based upon a case study of Lake Volta, Ghana in

1973 and 1974). Washington, D.C.: Smithsonian Institution, Office of International and Environmental Programs, 1974.

———. *The Environmental Impact of Rapid Urbanization: Guidelines for Policy and Planning,* (based upon a case study of Seoul, Korea in 1972 and 1973), Washington, D.C.: Smithsonian Institution, Office of International and Environmental Programs, 1974.

Goodland, R., and Tillman, G. *Guatemala National Energy Master Plan: Environmental Assessment.* New York: The Cary Arboretum of the New York Botanical Garden, December 1975.

Haas, Michael, ed. *The Asian Development Bank: Basic Documents of Asian Regional Organizations,* 1974.

Hafez, Moustafa. *The Environmental Impacts of the Aswan Dam.* U.N. Document E/CONF.70/TP/7. Cairo, Egypt: Ministry of Irrigation, Academy of Sciences Research and Technology, January 1977.

Hamilton, Lawrence S. *Tropical Rain Forest Use and Preservation: A Study of Problems and Practices in Venezuela.* Sierra Club Special Publication, International Series no. 4, March 1976.

Henderson, P.D. *India: The Energy Sector.* Washington, D.C.: International Bank for Reconstruction and Development, 1975. Council of Scientific Unions. *Arid Lands Irrigation in Developing Countries.* Paris: Scientific Committee on Problems of the Environment (SCOPE), 1977.

International Development Conference. *To Shelter Humanity: Summary Report.* Washington, D.C.: American University, November 1975.

International Institute for Environment and Development. *Human Settlements and National Reports: Summaries and Reference Guide.* New York: Pergamon Press, 1976.

International Union for Conservation of Nature and National Resources Secretariat. *Ecological Guidelines for Development in Tropical Forest Areas of Southeast Asia, Gandung, Indonesia.* Occasional Paper no. 10, Morges, Switzerland: International Union for the Conservation of Nature, 1974.

Jackson, Sir Robert. *A Study of the Capacity of the United Nations Development System* (Jackson Report). U.N. Document E.70.1.10 DP/5, Geneva: 1969.

Johnson, Brian. *The United Nations System and the Human Environment.* University of Sussex: Institute for the Study International Organization, 1971.

Kim, Byong Kuk. *Manual for Water Supply Project Appraisal,* Manila: Asian Development Bank, 1977.

———. *A Review of Bank Operations in Water Supply and Sewerage Sector* (September 1968-April 1976). Manila: Asian Development Bank, 1976.

Lauria, Donald T.; Kolsky, Peter; and Middleton, Richard N. *Design of Low-Cost Water Distribution Systems.* P.U. Report no. RES11, Washington, D.C.: International Bank for Reconstruction and Development, September 1977.

Levi, Lennart, and Anderson, Lars. *Population, Environment and Quality of Life: A Contribution to the UN World Population Conference.* London: Royal Ministry for Foreign Affairs, 1972.

Man and the Biosphere (MAB). *Expert Panel on Project No. 1: Ecological Effects of Increasing Human Activities on Tropical and Sub-Tropical Forest Ecosystems in the Programme on Man and the Biosphere.* Final Report no. 3. Paris: May 1972.

McJunkin, Euguene F., ed. *International Program in the Environmental Aspects of Industrial Development.* Chapel Hill, N.C.: University of North Carolina, Department of Environmental Sciences and Engineering, 1975-1977.

McNamara, Robert S. "Address to the Board of Governors of the World Bank." Nairobi, Kenya, 24 September 1973.

_____. "Address to the Board of Governors of the World Bank." Manila, Philippines, 4 October 1976.

_____. "Address to the Massachusetts Institute of Technology." Cambridge, Mass., 28 April 1977.

Mohammed, Kamal Ali. *The Projects for the Increase of the Nile Yield with Special Reference to Jonglei Project.* U.N. Document E/CONF.70/TP 30, 17 January 1977.

Munn, R.E., ed. *Environmental Impact Assessment: Principles and Procedures.* Scientific Committee on Problems of the Environment, Report no. 5, Toronto, Canada: Scientific Committee on Problems of the Environment (SCOPE), 1975.

National Academy of Sciences. *Energy for Rural Development: Renewable Resources and Alternative Technologies for Developing Countries.* Washington, D.C.: National Academy of Sciences, 1976.

_____. *More Water for Arid Lands: Promising Technologies and Research Opportunities,* Report of an Ad Hoc Panel of the Advisory Committee on Technology Innovation, Washington, D.C.: National Academy of Sciences, 1974.

Palmedo, Philip F., et al. *Energy Needs, Uses, and Resources in Developing Countries.* Upton, N.Y.: National Center for Analysis of Energy Systems, Brookhaven National Laboratory, March 1978.

Pereira de Silva, Alberto, and Mathe, Robert E. *Environmental Factors to be Incorporated into Existing Sector Guidelines.* Washington, D.C.: Inter-American Development Bank, November 1973.

Powers, Terry A. *Guidelines for Appraising Urban Potable Water Projects.* Paper on Project Analysis no. 4, Washington, D.C.: Inter-American Development Bank, Economic and Social Development Department, February 1977.

Program for International Development, *The Environmental Context of Development in Tanzania: A Map of Environmental Pressure Points.* Project Document 12223.3, Massachusetts: Clark University, Frebruary 1977.

Rockefeller Foundation. *Conference on International Development Strategies for the Sahel.* May 1975.

Saunders, Robert, and Warford, Jeremy. *Alternative Approaches to Sanitation Technology.* World Bank Progress Report, Research Project 671-46, Washington, D.C.: International Bank for Reconstruction and Development, January 1978.

Schneider, Hartmut. *National Objectives and Project Appraisal in Developing Countries.* Paris: Organization for Economic Cooperation and Development, 1975.

Stein, Jane. *Water: Life or Death.* Report in preparation for the United Nations Water Conference, March 1977, Washington, D.C.: International Institute for Environment and Development, 1977.

Stoel, Thomas B.; Scherr, S. Jacob; and Crowley, Diana C. "Environment, Natural Resources, and Development: The Role of the US Agency for International Development." Washington, D.C.: National Resources Defense Council, 1978.

Tillman, R., and Goodland, R. *National Power Study Pre-Feasibility Investigation: Environmental Impact Reconnaissance.* New York: The Cary Arboretum of the New York Botanical Garden, 1975.

United Nations. *Report of HABITAT, United Nations Conference on Human Settlements.* UN Document A/CONF.70/15, 1976.

_____. *Report of the United Nations Water Conference.* U.N. Document E/CONF.70/29, 1977.

United States Agency for International Development. *Environmental Assessment guidelines Manual.* Washington, D.C.: U.S. Agency for International Development, 1974.

U.S., Congress, House, Committee on Appropriations. *Foreign Assistance and Related Agencies Appropriations for 1978, Hearings* before a subcommittee of the Committee on Appropriations of the U.S. House of Representatives, (Part 1). 95th Congress, 1st sess., 1976.

U.S., Congress, Senate, Commerce Committee. *Survey of Environmental Activities of International Organizations, Hearings* before the Commerce Committee of the U.S. Senate. 92nd Congress, 2nd sess., 1972.

Ward, Barbara. Prologue to *Clean Water For All: a Seminar at Habitat United National Conference on Human Settlements.* Washington, D.C.: International Institute for Environment and Development, 1976.

White, Gilbert. *Water Supply Service for the Urban Poor: Issues.* P.U. Report no. PUN31, Washington, D.C.: International Bank for Reconstruction and Development, August 1977.

Official Documents of the Institutions Studied

African Development Bank. *Cooperation with the National Development Finance Institutions.* 1967.

_____. *First Annual Meeting of the Board of Governors: Proceedings*. Rabat, July 1974.

_____. *Five Years Forward*. 1970.

_____. *Loans and Investments: Statement of Policy and Procedure*. 1967.

Arab Bank for Economic Development of Africa. *Bilateral and Multilateral Arab Finance Institutions*. 1976.

_____. *Financial Regulations*. 1976.

_____. *General Agreement Establishing the Arab Bank for Economic Development of Africa*. 1976.

_____. *Principles Governing the Bank's Policy on the Financing of Development Projects in Africa*. 1976.

_____. *Rules Governing the Finance Operations of the Bank*. 1976.

Asian Development Bank. *Annual Meeting of the Board of Governors: Summary of Proceedings*. Manila, 1968.

_____. *Annual Report,* 1967-1975, inclusive.

_____. *Appropriate Technology and its Application in the Activities of the Asian Development Bank*. Occasional Paper, no. 7. April 1977a.

_____. *Basic Information*. 1971.

_____. *Informal Framework for Environment/Development Planning—National and Regional Levels*. April 4, 1977b.

_____. *Questions and Answers*. 1976.

The Caribbean Development Bank. *Annual Report*. 1970-1976, inclusive.

_____. *Basic Information*. April 1976 and May 1977.

_____. *By-Laws of the Caribbean Development Bank*. Approved by the Board of Governors at the Inaugural Meeting, 31 January 1970.

_____. *The Caribbean Development Bank and Industrial Development*. 1974.

_____. *Financial Policies*. 1970

_____. *Guidelines for Choice of Consultants*. 1971.

_____. *Guidelines for Procurement*. 1973.

_____. *Special Development Fund Rules*. (Current.)

The European Development Fund. Assemblee Parlementaire Europeenne, *Recommendation Adoptee par la Conference de l'Assemblee Parlementaire Europeenne avec les Parlements d'Etats Africans et de Madagascar le 24 juin 1961*. 26 juin 1961.

_____. European Communities Commission. *Balance Sheets of the European Development Funds for the . . . Financial Year* (beginning with 1974 financial year).

_____. *The Conditions Under Which Aid is Implemented and Used by the Recipient Associated States, Countries and Territories*. 1973-1976.

_____. *European Development Fund—Breakdown by Nationality of Contracts Financed by the EDF*. 1967-1976.

_____. *Evaluation Criteria for Projects Submitted to the European Development Fund Studies*. Overseas Development Series, no. 3. 1966.

_____. *Execution des projets finances par le Fonds European de developpement recueil des instructions.* 1970.

_____. *Financement et execution des projets,* (1962-1964). Situation des projets an execution (1965-present).

_____. *Situation semestrielle des projets due 2eme Fed an execution.* 1967-1975 inclusive.

_____. *Second Action Program on the Environment.* R670 e/77 (env 36).

_____. European Communities Council. *Internal Agreement on the Measures and Procedures Required for Implementation of the ACP–EEC Convention of Lome.* 1975.

The International Bank for Reconstruction and Development, *Agricultural Land Settlement.* A World Bank Issues Paper. January, 1978.

_____. *Annual Reports,* World Bank and International Development Association. 1967-1977.

_____. *Appropriate Technology for Water Supply and Waste Disposal,* Progress Report. June 1977.

_____. *The Assault on World Poverty: Problems of Rural Development, Education and Health.* Preface by Robert S. McNamara. A World Bank Paper. Balitmore: The Johns Hopkins University Press, 1975.

_____. *Curricula of Courses September 1975 to August 1976 and Catalog of Teaching Materials.* Economic Development Institute, Teaching Materials and Publications Unit. December 1976.

_____. *Development Finance Companies.* Sector Policy Paper. April 1976.

_____. *Energy and Petroleum in Non-OPEC Developing Countries.* World Bank Staff Working Paper no. 229. February 1976.

_____. *Environment and Development.* June 1975.

_____. *Environment, Health and Human Ecologic Considerations in Economic Development Projects.* 1974.

_____. *Forestry.* Sector Policy Paper, Agricultural and Rural Development Department. March 1978.

_____. *Guidelines for Procurement Under World Bank Loans and IDA Credits.* August 1975.

_____. *Health.* Sector Policy Paper. March 1975.

_____. *Health Aspects of Excreta and Sullage Management* (Draft). December 1977.

_____. *IDA, General Conditions Applicable to Development Credit Agreements.* March 1974.

_____. *IDA, General Conditions Applicable to Loan and Guarantee Agreements.* March 1974.

_____. *Measurement of the Health Benefits of Investments in Water Supply.* P.U. Report no. 20. 1977.

_____. *Minerals and Energy in the Developing Countries.* May 1977.

_____. *Nepal: Forestry Subsector Paper.* March 1975.

_____. *Operation Manual*. (Current.)

_____. *Operations Evaluation, World Bank Standards and Procedures*. June 1976.

_____. *Policies and Operations*. September 1974.

_____. *Questions and Answers*. March 1976.

_____. *Rural Development*. Sector Policy Paper. February 1975.

_____. *Rural Electrification*. Sector Policy Paper. October 1975.

_____. *Rural Enterprise and Non-Farm Employment*. A World Bank Paper. January 1978.

_____. *Sites and Services Projects*. A World Bank Paper. April 1974.

_____. *The Task Ahead for the Cities of the Developing Countries*. Staff Working Paper no. 209. July 1975.

_____. *Urban Transport*. May 1975.

_____. *Uses of Consultants by the World Bank and Its Borrowers*. April 1974.

_____. *Village Water Supply*. A World Bank Paper. March 1976.

_____. *Water Supply and Sewerage*. Sector Working Paper. October 1971.

_____. *The World Bank's Role in Schistosomiasis Control*. January 1978.

_____. *World Tables 1976. From the Data Files of the World Bank*. 1976.

Inter-American Development Bank. *Address of Antonio Ortiz Mena, President of the Inter-American Development Bank, before the UN Conference on the Human Environment*. Stockholm, Sweden: 12 June 1972.

_____. *Agreement Establishing the Inter-American Development Bank*. 1 June 1976, as amended.

_____. *Annual Reports*, 1960-1976 inclusive.

_____. *By-Laws*. 18 May 1975.

_____. *Economic and Social Progress in Latin America*. 1976.

_____. *Fifteen Years of Activities*, 1960-1974.

_____. *Fisheries Development in El Salvador*.

_____. *General Directions for Presenting Requests for Loans Destined to Finance Agricultural Development Projects*. April 1967.

_____. *Guide for Preparation of Feasibility Studies for Electric Power Projects* (revised draft). November 1977.

_____. *Guidelines for the Preparation of Projects for Highways*. Project Analysis Department, Division of Infrastructure, 1969.

_____. *Guidelines for the Preparation of Projects for Industrial Loans*. Division of Industry, 1973.

_____. *Guidelines for the Preparation of Projects for Port Facilities*. Project Analysis Department, Division of Infrastructure, 1970.

_____. *Guidelines of Information to be Furnished in Application for Industrial Loans*. July 1969.

_____. *Operational Policies Manual, Draft Section on Environmental Management*. October 1976.

_____. *Organizational Chart, Organizational Manual*. Supersedes September 1, 1976 Basic Organization. November 1976.

_____. *Participation of the Bank in the Development of Agriculture in Latin America.* Project Analysis Department, April 1977.

_____. *Regulations of the Board of Governors.* February 14, 1975.

_____. *Regulations of the Board of Executive Directors.* December 31, 1973.

_____. *Statement of Loans, 1975.*

_____. *Statement of Loans, 1976.*

Organization of American States. *Agriculture and Development.* Department of Information and Public Affairs, April 1973.

_____. *Annual Reports,* 1971-1975, inclusive.

_____. Centro Interamericano para el Desarrollo Regional (CINDER), *Seminario: El Manejo del Medio Ambiente y el Desarrollo Regional: El Caso de la Cuenca del Lago de Maracaibo.* April 1976.

_____. *Cuenca del Rio de la Plata: Estudio para su Planificacion y Desarrollo.* Department of Information and Public Afairs, 1971.

_____. *Environmental Quality and River Basin Development: A Model for Integrated Analysis and Planning.* Department of Regional Development, 1977.

_____. "In Defense of Nature." *Americas.* June-July 1973.

_____. *Physical Resource Investigations for Economic Development: A Casebook of OAS Field Experience in Latin America.* Department of Information and Public Affairs, 1969.

_____. *Programa de Desarrollo Regional.* Department of Information and Public Affairs, 1974.

_____. *Seven Years of Change: 1968-1975.* Department of Information and Public Affairs, 1975.

_____. Organization of American States, Program Interamericano de Formulación y Evaluación de Projectos (CETREDE). *Consideraciones Ambientales en la Formulacion y Evalua cion de Proyectos.* 1976.

_____. *Inter-American Program on Project Formulation and Evaluation.* 1976.

United Nations Development Programme. *Annual Report,* 1972-1975, inclusive.

_____. *Compendium of Approved Projects to 30 June, 1975* (UNDP/MIS/ Series/A no. 7). New York, September 1975.

_____. *Compendium of Approved Projects as of 30 June 1976* (UNDP/MIS/ Series/A no. 7). New York, September 1976.

_____. *Drought in Africa.* 1976.

_____. Governing Council, 1969. *Strenthening the Capacity of UNDP* (DP/L.134). June 9-26, 1970.

_____. Governing Council, 22nd Session. *The United Nations Capital Development Fund Annual Report 1975* (DP/182) April 1976.

_____. *Report of the Administrator,* 1972-1976, inclusive.

_____. *Reports of the Governing Council of the United Nations Development Programme.* Sessions 1322.

_____. *UNDP 1976-1977 and Beyond,* The Administrator's Report to the Governing Council. June 1977.

_____. United Nations Environment Programme, General Assembly, 30th Session. *UNEP Report of the Governing Council on the Work of its Third Session, 17 April to 2 May, 1975* (A/10/25). General Assembly Official Records, Supplement no. 25, 1975.

_____. General Assembly, 31st Session. *UNEP Report of the Governing Council on the Work of its 4th Session, 30 March to 14 April, 1976* (A/31/25). General Assembly Official Records, Supplement no. 25, 1976.

_____. Governing Council, 4th Session. *Eco-Development* (UNEP/GC/80). January 15, 1976.

_____. *Environment and Development* (UNEP/GC/76). January 20, 1976.

_____. *Environmental Impact of Irrational and Wasteful Use of Natural Resources* (UNEP/GC/79). January 23, 1976.

_____. *Review of the Impact of Production and Use of Energy on the Environment* (UNEP/GC/60). January 21, 1976.

_____. Governing Council, 5th Session. *Environment and Development Including Irrational and Wasteful Uses of Natural Resources of Eco-Development: Intergovernmental Impact Arising from Uses of Natural Resources* (UNEP/GC/102). March 7, 1977.

_____. *The State of the Environment* (GE 76-9368-6811). Switzerland, October 1976.

_____. *UNDP Projects with Environmental Implications.* Compiled by United Nations Environment Programme, 1976.

Index

About the Authors

Robert E. Stein has been director of the North American office of the International Institute for Environment and Development for the past four years, directing and participating in projects on marine environment and environmental assessment. He served on the Interagency Panel on Ocean Dumping, and has prepared expert testimony on sea disposal of radioactive waste. He also served as adviser to the United States delegation to the United Nations Water Conference and was a member of the Advisory Committee on the Law of the Sea. Mr. Stein has written or edited many articles, including "Critical Environmental Issues on the Law of the Sea" (IIED, 1975), and "Legal and Political Aspects of OTEC," in *Ocean Thermal Energy Conversion* (Lexington Books, D.C. Heath, 1977). He is currently executive director of Environmental Mediation International, a center for the resolution of environmental disputes.

Brian Johnson has written and lectured extensively on developmental and environmental issues, both in Europe and the United States. He is the former director of the Ecological Foundation, London, and of the Institute for the Study of International Organization at the University of Sussex, United Kingdom. He has held fellowships at Columbia University and Sussex University and is currently a senior fellow of the International Institute for Environment and Development. His books include *The Politics of Money* (McGraw-Hill, 1970); *Eco-Systems in Crisis* (1973); *Third World and Environmental Interests in the Law of the Sea* (IIED, 1974); and *Whose Power to Choose, International Institutions and the Control of Nuclear Energy,* (IIED, 1977).